To: My Lovely
friend HANNAH

CNT wait to
WEAR my!
HAT LOL!
£ FOR SHY
TO BE BRIDESMAID
flower girl ETC
get move on!
LOL

HOW TO PROPOSE

Love Jay

How to Propose

by

LANE SHEARER

---

365 Ways to Pop the Question

Martino Publishing
Mansfield Centre, CT
2012

Martino Publishing
P.O. Box 373,
Mansfield Centre, CT 06250 USA

www.martinopublishing.com

ISBN   978-1-61427-261-8

© *2012 Martino Publishing*

Cover design by T. Matarazzo

Printed in the United States of America On 100% Acid-Free Paper

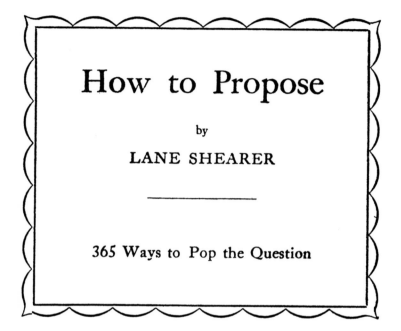

How to Propose

by

LANE SHEARER

365 Ways to Pop the Question

LARCH PUBLICATIONS
42 West 18th Street
New York, N. Y.

INTRODUCTION

There is no use pretending it isn't so. A girl's career is marriage. Any other career she takes up is either something to do while she waits for the right man to propose, or something to do after she has given up hope. Lots of girls propose to men, and they don't wait for February 29th, every four years, either; but the usual thing is still to let the man do the proposing, or rather to *get* the man to do the proposing. If and when our civilization is turned around backwards and the women support the men, it will be to man's advantage to learn how to inveigle girls into proposing. Until then it's up to the girl to make the opportunity for the man, get the family out of the way, hold his hand, fan his brow, put words into his mouth, ask leading questions, nudge, suggest, hint, imply, and finally faint with relief when he eventually gets the idea and pops the question. In general the old saying still holds true: "A man chases a woman until she catches him" and here are 365 ways in which he proposed.

The Editor

365 WAYS TO MAKE HIM PROPOSE

1. He took her to a Gypsy Tea Room. She was having her fortune told. Following a double line in her palm, the gypsy told her: "This is you and the man you love walking down the aisle together, and here where the two lines become one is an altar." She then looked up at Him and smiled. "Do you think there's anything in it?" She asked. "I know there is," He told Her; "just name the day."

2. He wrote Her a letter, and ended with this P. S.: "If I asked you to marry me, how would you get out of it?" She answered, and added this P.S. to her letter: "If I said Yes, how would *you* get out of it?" He didn't.

3. She was always being kidded about being fat, but she took it good naturedly and kidded right back. "The fellow that marries me," She told Him, "will have to hug half of me and then make a mark and hug the other half." "I'm willing to make two trips of it," He said immediately.

4. They were at the movies together, and He kept telling Her how crazy He was about Her; but he couldn't get His courage up to the point of asking Her to marry Him. Finally a man in the seat behind them leaned over and said: "Listen, you two, I paid to see a movie not a love-scene. This fellow loves you and

wants to marry you. Say yes and slide down and kiss him, so I can see the picture." She said yes.

5. She was a nurse, and was taking two children on the train. "Are the children half-fare?" She asked the young man who was selling the tickets. "Not half so fair as their nurse," He said. "Thank you," She said blushing. "I'll bet I could think up one like that every morning for years," He remarked. "What a pity I won't be there to hear them," She said. "Well, you could be if you wanted to," said He; and that was all there was to it.

6. They were having dinner in a little restaurant. Between courses He whispered: "I love you terribly, but marriage is a gamble, don't you think?" "Yes," She told Him, "but I'll be glad to take the chance."

7. She went to a masquerade as Martha Washington and danced with Robin Hood and The Shiek of Araby. Then George Washington cut in and She danced with Him for the rest of the evening. At midnight when the costumes were judged, they got the prize for the best couple. It was an odd amount, ending in a five, and they weren't sure how to divide it. "Why divide it at all," He suggested; "let's get married and keep it in the family."

8. He was afraid of mother-in-law trouble when He found that She was very devoted to Her mother. But He proposed anyway. "Do you think two can live as cheaply as one?" He

asked. "I suppose so," She countered; "do you think three can live as cheaply as two?" "Why not?" He answered; "it's one-third easier."

9. She was twenty-six, and had been going with Him for three years. He never seemed to be in a proposing mood, so she took the bit between Her teeth and said: "I don't see any point in our running around together all this time, do you?" "Why, I should say I do," He told Her. "This has just been practise for our running around together for the rest of our life, if you'll marry me."

10. They both had equally good jobs and they often went Dutch treat. "My girl-friends say I'm a chump for not making you pay all the time," She told Him one evening. "Don't you believe them," He told Her. "I love you for your fairness. But if you really want to stop, why not marry me, and then I'll pay all the bills."

11. She was a nurse and He was just getting out of the hospital. "Be careful not to over-exert yourself," She said; "or your stitches will all come out." "If you'd marry me, I'd have you around to sew me up again," said He.

12. He was tutoring Her in history over the summer vacation, and She passed the entrance exam in the fall with flying colors. "How can I ever thank you?" She asked Him. "By marrying me," He said quickly; "then you'll have a tutor around the house all the time if you need one."

13.   He was the breezy, talkative type. "Let's get married,"
He told Her one night. "All right, let's," She said. There was
a long silence. "Why don't you say something?" She asked.
"I've said enough already," said He.

14.   She believed in thought-transference and he didn't. "You
concentrate every night at nine o'clock while I'm gone," He told
Her before leaving on a trip out of town, "and see if you can
get the message I'll be transmitting." She concentrated reli-
giously, but finally had to write to Him: "All I ever seem to
hear is 'Will you marry me?'" "That's all you have to hear,"
He wrote back; "that's the message I've been sending."

15.   She liked hot-dogs, and used to have them every evening
at the delicatessen. One day the proprietor said to her: "You
like hot-dogs so much; why don't you buy them by the pound
and save money?" "Where would I cook them?" She asked.
"If you married me we'd have our own kitchen," He immediately told Her, " and I'd do all the cooking."

16.   They had only known each other a short time. "What do
you think of fellows who propose to girls after only knowing
them a week or two?" He asked. "Don't you think they're asking a lot of the girl?" "Not at all," She disagreed. "If I liked a
man well enough I'd jump at the offer no matter how soon he
made it." "Well, jump then," He smiled, "I'm leaving town
in ten days!"

17. He was a widower, and kept a housekeeper to look after the two children with which He had been left. When one of the children was taken sick, the housekeeper refused to let Him send the child to the hospital, and nursed the baby back to health all alone. "No mother could have done more," He told Her. "Why not marry me, and be the children's real mother?"

18. He was rather bashful and couldn't come right out and propose. "If a fellow my height and my weight and my age and my looks asked you to marry him, what would you do?" He finally asked. "I'd ask him if he had a twin brother," She said, "and if he didn't, it would be you, darling, and I'd marry you."

19. They had had a fight and were not speaking. Her kid brother was around enjoying the fun. "Listen, Arthur," He said to Her kid brother, while she sat right there listening to them, "If I give you a quarter will you ask your sister to marry me?" Arthur was willing and conveyed the message. "Tell him to save his money and ask me personally," She told the messenger. And the bargain was sealed with a kiss.

20. He had an artificial limb and had never told her, and wondered if a proposal under the circumstances would be honorable. "Could you marry a man that was missing a leg?" He asked her. "Why not," She countered, "as long as he wasn't missing a heart." Nothing else needed to be said.

21. She was worried about figuring out Her income tax, and

He was an accountant. "Let's get married," He suggested, "and then I'll do all the figuring." "I wasn't figuring on that," She said, "but it sounds wonderful."

22.   At a country dance and party a young man politely complimented the hostess on her excellent cake. "Oh, I didn't make that cake," the hostess said; "one of the girls brought it." "Well, I'm going to marry the girl who baked this cake," He announced, and went around the room asking every girl until he came to Her.

23.   In some busy offices not all letters are read. Only every fifth one got attention in Her office She told Him. The next day she got five letters, all identical. The message: "Darling, Please marry me. I'm sending this in quintuplicate, to make sure no business practice keeps you from reading this."

24.   They were both interested in books, and every time He went to see Her, He brought some de luxe copy or finely bound book as a present. One day She remonstrated: "You must stop giving me your books, or soon you won't have any library left yourself." "That's all right," He told Her, "I'm plotting to marry you, and then all the books will be *our* library."

25.   Not all girls get their men by being wonderful cooks. She was one of the world's worst, but she kept trying hopefully, and He kept eating Her cooking to be polite. One day though, after a lunch composed of canned fruit-juice, burned meat-loaf, biscuits like rocks, soggy salad, and bitter coffee, He took Her in

His arms and said: "Darling, they're going to take back my life insurance if I keep eating your cooking. Let's get married and both keep working. Then we can afford to eat in restaurants."

26.   He came to visit Her one evening with Her six-year-old son in tow. "I found him planning to join the Foreign Legion," He said. "Yes," volunteered the little boy; "since Daddy 'went away' I'm tired living in this old house with just women around." "That's what I've been trying to tell your Mother," He said, "That what this house needed was another man in it." "You're both against me," she sighed. "I guess I'll have to say yes."

27.   They were both raised on the farm, but He had an ambition to go to town. "If you wait, darling," He told Her, "I'll come back rich and a business-man, and I'll marry you then." She let Him underline his offer with a kiss and then told Him: "I'd like it better if you stayed poor and a farmer, and married me now." And that's just what He did.

28.   She was hurt in an automobile accident when she swerved the family car to avoid hitting a child who ran out in the street after a ball. He went to see her in the hospital, and sat there silently by her bed. "Cheer up," She told Him, "I'll be better soon." I know you will, sweetheart," He said. "What I was thinking of was: if you take that much care of somebody else's baby to risk your life for it, just think how you'd love *our own* baby."

29.   She worked for the same company He did, but in another part of the office-building.   Every time He wanted to see Her, it was a matter of walking about three blocks through winding corridors and up and down stairs.   Finally He decided He had had enough of that, and sent Her an inter-office memo: "Present method of seeing you very inefficient. Waste time and shoe-leather.   Imperative that you marry me, so I can see you any time I want, without all this red-tape."

30.   Not every young man is so brisk.   Another chap was so bashful that He was tongued-tied when with Her, but the minute He got home He put down on paper all the beautiful things He just couldn't get up enough courage to say on the spot.   He would sit up half the night writing, and His room-mate couldn't get a proper night's sleep on account of the light burning till all hours.   Finally, in desperation, the room-mate stole one of those beautiful letters and mailed it without His knowledge, something He had never gotten up courage to do. She accepted by return mail.

31.   She was the ditto-machine operator, and always used to say "Ditto" by way of agreeing with something.   One day, to break Her of the habit, He said: "I'll bet I can ask you three things you won't say 'ditto' to." "I'll bet you can't," She retorted. "I love you," He said. "Ditto," said She. "I want to marry you." "Ditto." "And I'm going to marry you!" "Ditto, darling!"

32. He used to see her every Saturday night, but one week all His friends were going to a basket-ball game, and He called Her up to ask: "Do you mind if I see you next Saturday night; I'd like to go to the game with the gang tonight." "I haven't the right to tell you where to go and where not to go," She said. "I'd like to give you that right," He said. She accepted, and He decided not to go to the basket-ball game that night.

33. She was making supper for Him, and they got so interested in kissing that the toast burned. "That's the last piece of bread in the house, too," she wailed. "Dearest," He told Her, "I'd rather eat burned toast with you for one night than eat fried hummingbirds with Venus DeMilo for the rest of my life." "That's just what you're going to do," She said. "How about letting me make a life-time career of it?" He asked.

34. They were horse-back riding, and Her horse threw Her. She wasn't hurt but She had to ride back sitting behind Him on the one horse. Every time He twisted around to try to kiss Her, they nearly fell off. "I'll bet if we were married you wouldn't think a kiss was worth falling off a horse for," She told Him. "I'll just bet I would," He replied. "And I'll bet you wouldn't," She insisted. "Well," He said after a pause, "there's only one way to find out."

35. He was a blood-donor, and She needed a transfusion. After She was better, She insisted on looking Him up and thanking Him personally. They went out a few times and got to

know each other well. Finally He said: "Seeing that you have some of my blood in you, I think I ought to marry you and keep it in the family." She was willing.

36.   He was a one-woman man, and it hurt Him terribly when She went out with someone else. "Isn't there any way of taking you out of circulation besides marrying you?" He finally asked in desperation. "Would that be your only reason?" She countered. "Well, it would be one of the best," said He; "how about it?"

37.   Her family did not like Him, so He couldn't come to Her house. His family would have been shocked if She came to His house. "If I'm ever going to see you," He said, "we'll have to get a house of our own." So they did.

38.   They were talking about money. "If I had a lot of money, I'd ask you to marry me," He told Her. "Why wait until then?" She asked. "If you don't care, I won't" He agreed. "Will you marry me?" "I'll tell the world I will," She said.

39.   He was coming to visit Her, and as She sat waiting there was a horrible crash. She ran to look, and there He was, sitting on the stairs, rubbing His anatomy. "I fell," He said, rather unnecessarily "but I didn't get hurt." "How many stairs did you have left to climb?" She laughed. "They say that's how many years you have to wait before you get married." "Well then

we re going to be married right away," said He, "because I slipped on the top stair."

40. They were walking through the park one day, and stopped off at the bird-house. The love-birds caught their attention, and He said: "Did you know that if one of them dies the other one pines away and dies too?" "Would you do a thing like that?" She asked. "I can't help myself," He told Her, "I'm crazy about you. Maybe I'd better marry you and look after your health, just to be on the safe side."

41. Fried chicken was on the menu, so they ordered one. "Which part of the chicken do you prefer?" She asked when it was served. "If you're talking about the one on the dish, I like the leg best," He said, "but when it comes to a 'chicken' like you, I can't decide. Marry me, and then when I'm good and used to you ask me again."

42. His mother suggested to Him that He ought to marry the girl he had been going with for so long. He told Her about it that night at the movies. "Isn't that a funny idea: us getting married?" He said. "No, I don't think it's so funny," She said. "That's all I wanted to know," He chortled; "when's it going to be?"

43. She was using Him for the 'victim' in practising Red Cross bandaging, and finally she had him splinted and slinged till he couldn't move a finger. "How long are you going to leave me

this way?" He asked. "Oh, until you propose to me," She told him jokingly. "Well then," He said, "consider yourself proposed to; and now either untie me or climb in here with me."

44.   She was the cashier in her father's restaurant, and He had their laundry business. One day they were figuring out which came to more, Her laundry bill or His food bill for the week, and it came out exactly even. "Why do we go through all this bookkeeping every week?" He asked. "Let's get married and that will straighten everything out."

45.   The apples looked so tempting as they walked down the country road that She had Him boost her up into the tree to pick a couple while the farmer wasn't looking. But a dog began to bark and She got so nervous that she fell out of the tree. He caught Her and they tumbled to the ground together. "I guess I fell for you," She said laughingly. "And I fell for you long ago," He told her putting His arms around Her; "when are you going to marry me?"

46.   She was sick and He called Her in the evening to see if He could bring Her anything "Yes, a newspaper," She said. When he handed Her the paper later He remarked: "You know, bringing home the paper to you each night is a habit I'd love to cultivate." And it was all settled.

47.   At a party they were playing "Truth Or Consequences." "What do you think of me?" She asked Him, but He refused to

answer and had to kiss the leg of a chair for a forfeit. Later She asked Him why He wouldn't answer. "Is what you think of me so terrible?" She wanted to know. "No," He told her, "it's just that I think you're the only girl I'll ever want to marry, and I didn't want to parade my feelings in front of all those people." "Here's your forfeit back," She said, and She sealed their engagement with a real kiss.

48. She was offered two jobs at once, and couldn't make up Her mind which one to take. When She asked His advice, He looked thoughtful. "If I were you I wouldn't take either job," He said. "Why? Have you a better idea?" She wanted to know. "I sure do," He said; "marrying me."

49. Her younger brother opened the automatic elevator door and found them kissing. "I suppose it's all right if you really love each other," he said nonchalantly. "Better than that," He remarked; "We're getting married." "That's the first time I've heard of it," She said. "Any objections?" He wanted to know. There were no objections.

50. They were on a picnic and it began to rain cats and dogs. They took refuge under a tree with broad branches and were cozy and dry while the rain swept up and down the landscape. "Isn't it nice being here so safe while it's so terrible outside?" said She. "Marry me, darling, and it will always be that way," He told her.

51. He was the careful type. "Honey," He inquired, "if I asked you to marry me, would you?" "I think I would," She replied. "Then I won't ask!" He laughed. The next night He asked the same question and She told Him "Definitely not!" rather angrily. So He proposed anyhow, and She accepted anyhow. "I was hoping you'd fool me that way," He said. "And I was hoping you'd fool me that way too," She admitted.

52. His expenses were paid through college by a family that had befriended Him, and it was taken for granted that He would show his gratitude by marrying their rather plain daughter when he was graduated. When the time came, He proposed, but to his amazement She turned Him down flat. "I don't want a husband that my family has bought and paid for," She said. "I'll wait for a man who loves me to come along." They split up and went out with others, but after two years He realized She was the only girl for Him, and he searched Her out and proposed to her again. This time she was glad to accept.

53. They were depositing some film for development at the corner drugstore, and the clerk asked: "Is that Miss or Mrs.?" "What do you say, darling," Her boy-friend chimed in, "shall we make it Mrs.?"

54. He was Her husband's best friend, and Her husband was killed in an accident. After the mourning period was over, and He had been a rock of strength to Her all through it, He said:

"Alice, let's get married and keep Bob's memory fresh together all our lives. You owe it to the children."

55.   Whenever he took her out She would suggest going to a free concert or for a walk in the park, or something else that wouldn't cost him any money. Finally He said: "You know, going out with you is saving me so much money that pretty soon I'll have enough to get married on." "That's just what I've been waiting for you to say," She replied immediately.

56.   She was angry at Him and called Him a pill. He was angry too, and called Her a headache. The combination made them both laugh, and then they weren't angry any more. "I guess we go together," He said. "Better keep me around permanently for that headache of yours."

57.   He had known Her years before and met Her one day, and they began talking over old times. "I've never enjoyed an afternoon more," He gushed, "than remembering back to that crush I had on you." "If we married I'll bet you wouldn't say that," She countered. "Try me," He replied, "and see."

58.   She was a writer and needed a man's name to use on a story for a virile magazine. "Use mine," He suggested. "Isn't that illegal?" She wondered. "Not if we're members of the same family," He assured Her, and that made everything all right.

59.   "Which would you save if you were on a sinking ship,"

She asked Him; "Dr. Eliot's Six-Foot Library of the World's Greatest Classics, or a blonde?" "Neither," He said; "I'd swim back to shore and kidnap you for life. How about it?"

60.   She met two brothers at a dance one night, and took an immediate shine to one of them. "If you're just playing around with her," said the rejected brother one evening to the accepted one, "tell me, because I'd seriously like to marry her." That put his brother on his toes, and He proposed the same night.

61.   She was visiting the young bride who had just moved in next door when their watch-dog chased Her up a tree. Her boy-friend was passing and chased the dog, and invited Her to jump down and He would catch Her. "People would talk if they saw me fall into your arms in broad daylight," She demurred. "Not if we were engaged they wouldn't talk," He assured her. She jumped.

62.   He hadn't seen her for months and took Her to the movies the night He came back. On the screen the actress was wearing a corsage. "Aren't they beautiful?" She whispered to Him. "Wait," He whispered back, "and I'll get you some." Before She could stop Him, He had moved down the aisle and was gone. He was gone a very long time, and when He finally came back and started pinning the corsage on Her, He couldn't manage it in the dark and She had to help. Then She found what was wrong. He was trying to pin the corsage to Her with an engagement ring. She was so happy she began to cry.

63.   They wanted to go out, but it began to rain.   "Weather only lasts a few days," He said, "but climate lasts for years.   I can't promise that the weather will always be sunny, but if you marry me the climate will always be as warm as my heart can make it."   They decided to stay indoors.

64.   He wanted to kiss Her, but She wouldn't.   "That's only for married people," She said, but He laughed at Her and convinced Her differently.   Time went on, and one day She wanted to kiss him, but He wouldn't.   "That's only for married people," He reminded Her; "what do you say we make it legal?"

65.   He was coming to see Her, and everything delayed him. He had to wait for the bus.   He had to wait for the streetcar. He had to wait for the knock on the door to be answered, as the bell was broken.   Then He had to wait for her to get dressed. Next He had to wait for the family to disappear.   When He finally got Her alone He was fit to be tied. "If I have to do all this waiting just to see you," He complained, "how will it be if I ever want to marry you.   Maybe I'd better marry you right now while you're here." So they eloped.

66.   They were sitting in the dark and he was smoking a cigarette which was the only visible object.   He kept making designs in the air with the red tip, and suddenly She realized that He was writing over and over: "Will you marry me?"   She took the cigarette from Him, and wrote: "Yes, yes, yes!"

67.   He had just been turned down by another girl, and so when He proposed to Her, She refused Him. "You'd just be marrying me on the rebound," She told Him, "and that wouldn't be fair to either of us." He went away then, and She didn't see Him again for months. One night He stormed in and seized Her in His arms and began kissing Her. "What's this all about?" She objected. "I was just over at the other girl's house kissing her," He said, "but it wasn't the same as this at all. You're the girl for me if you'll have me."

68.   She was a school-teacher and He was a bachelor and they were eating in a crowded restaurant. They made room for an elderly lady to sit with them, and when they were leaving the lady remarked: "It's nice seeing a married couple so in love. Most couples argue at meals." They laughed and looked at each other. "It's a good beginning," He told Her, "shall we go on from there together?"

69.   Hope-chests were all the rage, but She didn't have one, and when He asked her why, She told him that she was wait- ing till She could get a good one — real mahogany lined with cedar — or She didn't want one at all. The next week one just answering the description was delivered to her house, with a note inside from Him saying: "This is my hope-chest too. I hope you'll let it be the first piece of furniture for our home."

70.   He was a sailor, and in a hand-knit cap the comfort organi-

zation gave him He found a slip of paper with Her name and address and an invitation to write. They got to know each other and one day He said: "You know I'd marry you if I weren't afraid that you'd knit another cap and meet some other fellow the way you met me." The next letter He got from Her contained two broken knitting needles.

71.   They had quarreled during the winter, and when Valentine's Day came She got an enormous valentine from Him, with the question "Will you be my Valentine?" changed to "Will you be my Wife?"   "I know it ruins the rhyme," He had written underneath, "but the sentiment is all there, believe me."

72.   They were on a hike to an Echo Lake, and were amusing themselves shouting and waiting for the answer. "Shout 'no'," He told Her.   She did, and the echo replied after a pause. "Now shout 'yes'," She did, but before the echo could come back, He hurriedly asked: "Will you marry me darling?" And Her voice came back across the lake: "Yes!"

73.   They were at a wedding and She was feeling a little jealous as all unmarried girls do at weddings.   "Isn't the bride a dream?"   She whispered to Him.   "If you were the bride it would be a dream come true," He told Her; "if I were the groom."

74.   They were playing True or False, and she was getting all the answers wrong.   Finally He said: "I'll give you one last

question, and you'd better get the answer right. Is a certain fellow sitting right next to you going to marry you just as soon as you name the day?" "The answer is 'true,' " She replied, closing Her eyes and waiting for Him to kiss Her.

75.   They were stopped on the street by the Inquiring Reporter, who asked Her the questions first. Then the reporter turned to Him. "Will you give me your name please?" was the first question.   "No, I will not," He said unexpectedly; "I'm saving my name to give to this young lady just as soon as she'll agree to be my wife."

76.   He had been going with Her for several months, and one evening He spent several hours telling Her that He wasn't the marrying kind, that He loved them and left them, that a fellow was a fool to give up his independence, et cetera.   He went home at about two A. M., and just as she was about to crawl into bed her phone rang.   "It's me," He said ungrammatically, "I'm down at the corner drug-store.   I don't suppose I convinced you any better than I convinced myself.   I really am crazy about you.   Will you marry me?"

77.   The girls were playing the Hallowe'en game where each girl looks in a mirror in a darkened room and is supposed to see in it the face of the man she's going to marry.   She actually saw a face in the mirror, but it turned out to be a picture of the hostess's brother, which was on the piano.   She came out and

told the company, which included the brother. "Who am I to argue with the Hallowe'en ghosts?" He asked. "You'd better marry me, or something terrible might happen to both of us."

78.   He wanted to propose to Her but kept getting cold feet. One day at a radio theatre that featured a hypnotist, He egged Her to go up to the stage with Him. After She had been hypnotized He asked the hypnotist to tell Her to kiss Him. She responded perfectly. "Now ask her to marry me," He begged the hypnotist. At that She opened her eyes and said: "I'm not hypnotized a bit. Why don't you ask me yourself?" The audience roared.

79.   They were having a religious argument about whom Cain in the Bible had married. He maintained that Cain had married a gorilla, and She argued that no, he married his sister. Finally He said, "Who cares who Cain married. The question is: will *you* marry me?"

80.   She always insisted on going to visit married friends and relatives on her dates with Him, and He began to smell a put-up job. "Is it your idea to show me how happily married they all are?" He finally asked. She admitted it, and He went on: "Because now that I've met them all, I'm beginning to feel conspicuous, as the only unmarried man around. How about marrying me, and then people will use us for an example of wedded bliss." It worked out.

81. He was the judge at a baking contest, and He gave Her the prize even though Her entry was the worst looking cake there. The other girls began to murmur, and He held up His hand and said right out loud: "Ladies, please forgive my judgment. I know that cake is simply terrible, but I want to propose to her tonight, and I've got to get her in a good mood."

82. It was the 4th of July and He wanted to stay home on their date. "What's the matter with you," She asked, "don't you know today is a holiday?" "Sure I know," He answered. "A year from now it will be the first anniversary of the day we got engaged, if you stay home and give me a chance to propose."

83. Her little sister embarrassed her terribly by asking Him: "Why don't you kiss her like all Her other fellows do?" While She was blushing, He replied: "So other fellows kiss her, do they? I'd better marry her before one of them thinks of that too." She married him.

84. He was a widower and She was a widow, and His grown-up daughter was in love with Her son. He would visit politely but he refused to sanction the marriage. One day She asked him why. "Because," He explained, "when the children marry they will move away, and I will no longer have any excuse to visit you, and forget my loneliness in your loveliness." "Can't anything be done?" She smiled. "Only if you'll consent to make a double wedding of it," He replied.

85.   They were having a snowball fight one winter afternoon, when She hit Him on the ear with a very hard snowball. When He complained, She said: "I'm Hard-Hearted Hannah, so watch out for me." He grabbed Her and held Her down and began washing Her face with snow. "Maybe this will melt you down," He laughed, "and then you'll be willing to marry me." And He got snow all over His face as He kissed Her.

86.   They were on horseback and Her horse kept bobbing its head up and down. She tried to restrain it, but the horse kept on. "Maybe it's trying to tell me what you'd say if I asked you to marry me," He suggested. The horse nodded again, very violently, and that settled it.

87.   They were always fighting whenever they met, and their friends marked the violent antipathy they seemed to have for each other. One day while they were arguing bitterly at a party where they ran into each other, someone asked loudly: "Why don't you two get married and do your fighting in private?" They both began to laugh, and before three months were past they had taken the advice. That kind of unreasonable hate usually turns out to be love.

88.   His name was John Alden, (You may have read about Him in history books) and He was trying to convince a girl named Priscilla that She ought to marry His best friend, Captain Miles Standish. Captain Standish was the finest this and the

finest that, He assured Her, and any girl would be lucky to be Captain Standish's wife. Finally She looked up from Her spinning and said to Him with a twinkle in Her eye: "Why don't you speak for yourself, John?"

89. He was always saying that He would only marry some rich girl for her money, and one day He did meet a rich girl. He fell in love with Her, but when He proposed She refused Him because friends had told Her that He was just a fortune-hunter and admitted it publicly. He borrowed three hundred dollars and went to Mexico and gambled it all on roulette. He went broke twice, but finally He hit the run of luck He had dreamed of and came back with eleven thousand dollars to prove He wasn't after Her money and to marry Her anyway. It came in very handy because Her father had lost all his money meanwhile, and She was looking for some rich fellow to marry.

90. He bought her a gorgeous lapel-watch for Christmas. It had ten diamond chips in it, and they were lovely. "How can I ever thank you?" She asked, when He had finally convinced Her that She ought to take it. "Oh, give me a kiss for each diamond," He said carelessly. "Fair enough," She said, and began paying Him, but He stopped Her after the first kiss. "I'll collect them one every Christmas," He said, "and just to make sure where you'll be, for the next ten years at least, maybe I'd better marry you."

91. She wanted to know what the "Four Freedoms" were. He

told Her, and then added: "There's a Fifth Freedom too — freedom from loneliness, furnished rooms, restaurant cooking, makeshift mending and kissless nights. How about doing your duty to your country and saving me from all that by marrying me?"

92.   They had gone around so long together that She could no longer wait for Him to propose at His own good time. One night in the shopping and amusement district, she kept steering him in to store windows to look at white dresses. "What is it about white dresses that appeals to you so?" He finally asked. "I don't know," She answered, "unless it's that they remind me of wedding gowns." He took the hint.

93.   They were at a lecture where the speaker said that married couples weren't really in love with each other after the first eight or ten years, but were simply used to each other. "I don't believe a word of it," She stormed on the way home. "Well," He said, "there's only one way to know for sure. Marry me and see."

94.   He was an orphan and had been going around with her for three years. One night at Her home He was filling out an application for a job, and when He came to the question "Next of kin?" He was stumped. "Can I use your name?" He asked Her. "Sure," She agreed, "if you don't think it will get you in trouble." "Maybe I'd better play safe and marry you," He suggested.

95.   He worked at the same factory She did, and obviously
had a terrible crush on Her. He began dropping things, and
lathing materials all crooked, until the foreman introduced
Him to Her just to preserve company property. After they had
gone together a while, He was observed to be getting careless
with His machine again, while He ogled Her across the plant.
Finally the foreman came over to Her and said: "If you like
that dopey boy-friend of yours, you better marry him and let
him get you out of his system, or I'll have to fire you both for
obstructing production."

96.   She was redecorating Her apartment when He came to
visit and She let Him sit down in a freshly painted chair without thinking.   When He wanted to get up He was stuck.
"Well," He laughed, "if I've got to stay here all my life, we'd
better get married or the neighbors will gossip."   She decided
that would be better than sawing the chair off him.

97.   She was a New Yorker and He was from Chicago, where
they met. After a few months She began telling Him all about
the opportunities She was sure He could find in New York, and
that He ought to go there. "What are you trying to do," He
asked; "get rid of me?" "No," She said, "I'm trying to hold
onto you; I'm being transferred back to New York, and I'm trying to sell you the idea of coming along."   "Why not marry
me and stay here?"   He countered.

98.   Her parents were very strict about Her getting home from dates early. She was very much in love with Him, and the time just slipped away, and suddenly it was midnight. "I have to go home," She fumed; "but for two cents I'd get married, and then I could do as I pleased." "It's a bargain," He said, and handed her two cents. "I only hope the upkeep will be as reasonable as the original investment."

99.   They were caught in the rain while on a walk on the edge of town, and they ducked into an abandoned quarry tower. "If you weren't here I could take my dress off and dry it," She remarked. "Or you could turn your back," She added. "Or we could get married," He countered. "I don't think that would take care of the proprieties right now," She laughed, "but it's a wonderful thought."

100.   He was kissing Her goodnight on Her doorstep and was putting all His love and passion into it. "Oh, darling," She said in a strangled voice; "I wish we could keep doing this forever." "Maybe we ought to get married while we're at it," He suggested, "and then we could do it sitting down."

101.   He told the young lady of his choice that, being the youngest of seven children, He was tired of living in such a crowded atmosphere and was going to leave for some other city where He could have a little room. "I'd go with you," She said, "but when I get married I intend to have ten kids. Maybe

we'd better not write to each other." "I wouldn't mind that kind of a crowded atmosphere," He answered Her.

102. They both owned dogs, and were accustomed to taking the dogs walking at about the same hour. Since the dogs were of the same breed, They did not object to the ripening friendship between the two animals, which were of opposite sexes. Then She had to move out of the neighborhood. "Spotty will miss seeing Prince every day," She told Him, "she's gotten very fond of him." "Maybe we'd better get married," He suggested, "and give them a home together."

103. He worked in a grocery store, and found an egg one day with a girl's name and address on it, and an invitation to write. The address was nearby, and instead of writing, He went out one Sunday afternoon. "No," a young lady told Him at that address, "Miss Hackett doesn't live here any more. She got married fourteen years ago, for the third time. She's my grandmother." The young man was startled, and told about the cold storage egg. "I wonder if anybody nowadays can store up an emotion as long as Grandma has," mused the girl. "I'll bet I could," He opined, "if the emotion was love for you." They were married within three months.

104. He was a telephone lineman and in the hospital because of an accident on the job. She was a nurse and asked how it happened. "I threw a ground loop over the haulaway," He

told Her, "but that damn fool on the clog let it winch, and it broke my leg." "I don't quite understand," She said. "Stick around," He told Her, "and I'll teach you the language." "I'm afraid you might throw a ground-loop over me," She smiled, "and break my leg." "Not on your life," He told Her. "Wait until I'm out of this cast and I'll dance you up the aisle in a church, just to show you how it's done."

105.   He was on his knees, trying to propose in the worst way, and that's the way He was doing it.   She was in a hammock in front of Him, trying to help things along.   When She saw that He was completely stuck for words, She loosened the rope at one end and was duly dumped on top of Him.   He clutched at Her wildly, and muttered, "All right, I'll marry you; you don't have to get sore about it."   (Sealed with a kiss.)

106.   She could only remember the last line of the newest popular songs, and He could only remember the opening bars. One night noticing how they helped each other through song after song, He stopped Her song by kissing Her, and said: "Darling, it takes both of us to make things complete.   When are you going to marry me and make things perfect for life?"

107.   They were at the circus and he bought her a gilt wooden copy of the "Tallest Man In the World's" wedding ring for a bracelet.   "I know it looks like a bracelet," He said, "but if you want to call it a wedding ring, so do I."

108. He was an automobile salesman and she was a difficult customer. One night He took Her out in His car, and said: "Lady, this is a bargain that only comes once in a lifetime. One super-duper, singing-bird, inlaid, supercharged, extra ultra heart full of love for you. With four new tires, and a hundred year guarantee. No down payment. What do you say?" She said yes.

109. They lived on opposite sides of a toll bridge and it cost them ten cents to cross over and see each other. "One of us might move across the river," She suggested, "think of the money we'd save that way." "Why not both of us get married," He countersuggested, "and then we'd have something worth saving money for?"

110. His girl's best girl-friend married a new fellow in town after going with another man for three years. "Why did Jean marry that chap so quickly?" He asked her one night. "I thought she was in love with somebody else." "I suppose because he asked her," She answered soberly. "No girl likes to wait forever, you know." Deep silence for a while, then He said. "Considering that we've been going together longer than Jean went with her first fellow, maybe I'd better propose before you marry the next stranger that moves into town."

111. Sometimes that sort of knock-down-and-drag out hint isn't necessary. The absent treatment works too. He had taken

up years of Her time as "steady boy-friend" without ever mentioning marriage. So one summer She took her vacation somewhere else from where He did. When She came back He was waiting at the station. "I guess you're in my blood after all this time," He told Her. "It was torture while you were gone. Let's get married and never separate again."

112. He had to break a date with Her, and She was ripping angry. He rushed over to Her house as soon as He could make it, but She would hardly speak to Him, and then only to be angry, while He apologized. Finally She burst out with: "Well, I certainly would never marry a man like you!" "Don't tell me you're going to refuse before I even ask you," He retorted. "Because if you're in such a hurry I'd better propose right away."

113. They were watching the moon one night, waiting for a predicted eclipse. When the strange blackness settled over the dead white orb, they both felt strangely morose. "Let's never let anything blot out our happiness that way," He said to Her quietly. "Let's get married and make every day full moon."

114. He had been dating her for several months. In all that time He and She never seemed to agree on anything. They argued about the weather, the affairs of the world, the character of their friends, the places they should go to. One evening He remarked "Is there anything I'd say that you'd agree to?" "Well, you haven't said it yet," she countered. He replied, "I think

you'll make a fine wife for me." She agreed.

115.   They heard church bells ringing one afternoon, a whole complicated chime, and very beautiful.   "Somebody must be dead," She suggested.   "They never ring the bells that way except on important occasions."   "Well, why a funeral?" He asked. "A wedding would be important too.   Especially," He added after a moment, "our wedding."

116.   She was on Her knees cutting out a dress pattern on the floor when He came to visit.   He knelt down with Her and took the scissors and a piece of newspaper.   "Let me make a pattern for you," He said.   And He cut out the letters: BE MY WIFE.

117.   He carried her books to school for her when they were both children.   Now, they were both grown up and working for the same firm.   On New Year's Eve the firm gave a party for all its employees.   Cocktails were served.   When she lifted her glass he took it out of her hand and set it down.   When she asked for an explanation for such behavior he said, "I don't want my future wife to drink in public."   "Is this a proposal?" She asked.   "It is," he replied.

118.   He worked for a shopping service and She worked in an office.   So they were in the funny situation of having Him, a man, doing the shopping for Her, a woman.   He got to know Her well, delivering small items to Her office every once in a

while. Ana one day He said, "Couldn't you arrange to marry me, and do the shopping for me for a while. This topsy-turvy arrangement is beginning to make me nervous."

119.   They were at an architectural exhibit, and the electrical dough-roller amazed Him. "What, no more rolling pins?" He asked Her. "What will Maggie beat up Jiggs with?" "Wives only hit their husbands with rolling pins in the funny papers," She told Him, laughing. "That's all I need to know," He laughed back. "Now I can ask you to marry me without worrying."

120.   Her favorite brother died, and She was all broken up at the funeral. "I couldn't hope to take the place of a real blood relative," He told Her on the ride back, "but if you'll marry me, I'll try to be all a brother could be and more."

121.   Sometimes a man can propose without saying a word to the girl. He took her into a jewelry store to buy Her a Christmas present. She had her eye on a brooch but He picked out something at the ring counter and called her over to look at it. "How much is that engagement and wedding-ring set?" He asked the jeweler. She slipped Her hand in His, and that was all there was to it.

122.   He was the boss, and She was just a steno. He had taken out most of the stenos, but they had irritated Him by agreeing with Him and yessing Him in everything, in hopes of promo-

tion to secretary. She was different, though. She argued with him the whole evening through. Intrigued, he took Her out again. She refused to treat Him like the boss after hours, and stood right up to Him. "I admire your spunk," He told Her finally. "We'll probably go from arguments to blows within a month, but I'll take the chance if you will. This is a proposal."

123. She knew He was an orphan, and so She was surprised when one day He announced He was planning to add another relative to the one He had. "What one have you?" She asked. "My Uncle Sam," He told her cheerily. "And you're going to be the other relative — my wife."

124. He was shy and felt He was too old for Her. It was New Year's Eve of Leap Year and when the whistles blew She asked Him: "Did any girl ever propose to you in a Leap Year." "I should hope not," He said flatly. "I'm man enough to do my own proposing." "Are you?" She asked simply. So he proposed.

125. He was always being kidded by mutual friends for not proposing to Her, as they had been going together for years. "When I do propose to her," He said, "the whole world will know about it." And He as right. He sent Her a telegram, asking her to marry Him, and tipped the messenger boy to tack

the telegram up on the bulletin board in the office, where everyone could read it.

126.   His parents had been very unhappy together and were
divorced.   Her home life was a picture of happiness, and He
used to come over several nights a week.   After several months,
He took the opportunity when Her parents had gone out one
night to say: "If I married you, would your family adopt me?"
"We've adopted you already, dearest," She told Him.   "And
they love you as much as I do."

127.   She had the apartment above His, and when hanging
Her wash out clothespins and hankies would always be
dropping and He'd bring them up to Her or She'd go down to
retrieve them.   One day a pair of panties fell down, and He
pretended to be embarrassed.   "I don't think I could hand an
intimate garment like this to anyone but my wife," He called
up to Her.   "If you want it back you'll have to marry me."

128.   He was an Inquiring Reporter, and She ran a newsstand
in the building.   Whenever typical people to interview were
scarce, He would put Her on the air, introducing Her by a different name each time.   One day He terrified Her when She was
being interviewed by saying: "I understand you made a false
statement about yourself."   And as She stood there petrified,
He added: "You said you were single and unattached. You may
not know it, but you're as good as married right now.   To me."

Later He confessed that the microphone had not been connected.

129.   They had had a foolish quarrel, and She refused to see Him.   He stood outside her house but She pulled down the shades.   Finally she heard noises and peeked.   There was a big crowd watching Him, and He was writing on the sidewalk with chalk, all around Her house.   She got opera glasses and read what He was writing: I LOVE YOU. I LOVE YOU. PLEASE MARRY ME.   P. S.   I LOVE YOU. She got a black cardboard and wrote on it in big letters and stood it in the window where He could see what it said, namely: YES, YOU IMBECILE. COME INSIDE BEFORE YOU GET ARRESTED.

130.   They both wanted to go on the stage, but Fame did not seem to beckon.   "I don't think we've suffered enough to be real actors yet," He told Her.   "Let's get married.   I have a terrible temper and will make you miserable.   Then you can divorce me and become a great actress."   "But what about you," She laughed.   "Oh, I'll be miserable because you're gone, and then I'll be a great actor too."

131.   He had been taking her out for several months, but had never bought her a gift.   One day she commented on it.   He replied, "I'll only buy gifts for the one I'll marry."   When next he called her up she said she was too busy to see him that night. He called her up the following night, and she again said she

was too busy. On the third night she said she would only go
out with the man who would be her husband. Within the hour
he came, bearing a huge gift of red roses.

132.   He was rather short, but She never kidded him about it.
"Darling," He told Her one night. "I'm just a shrimp, and I
know it even if you've never mentioned it. But if you'll marry
me I'll show you that I have a man-sized love for you." "I
never doubted it," She assured Him, as He hugged Her.

133.   They were playing Blind Man's Buff at a party, and He
found Her unerringly every time. "You're cheating," She
whispered to Him. "You can see out under the bandage." He
whispered back: "To get you I'd do more than cheat. I'd steal
bars of gold out of the sub-treasury in a market-basket. Will
you marry me and save me from a life of crime?"

134.   She tried to rush Him into popping the question and He
countered by getting a job out of town. Just as She was kicking Herself for scaring Him away She got a note from Him,
saying: "This town is perfect for a honeymoon. What do you
say?"

135.   They were at Her home eating Christmas dinner, and He
was pretending to be Her little sister's boy-friend. The little
sister took it all very seriously. "If you're my boy-friend," she
said, "You've got to kiss me." He kissed her. "Now that you
kissed me, you've got to marry me," the little girl went on.

Everybody burst out laughing then and He told her gravely: "I'd like to, but I'm planning on marrying your sister first. Better kiss somebody else now."

136.   He bragged to His friends about how wonderfully She could cook, so to avoid being caught short She pestered Her mother into teaching her the rudiments of cooking, so She could cook a dinner for His friends.   Then it turned out that they couldn't come, and She was very disappointed and told Him what She had done.   "Well," He told Her, "seeing that you went and learned to cook just to back me up, I think I ought to back you up and marry you, so your knowledge won't go to waste."

137.   She was quick-tempered, but He was slow and easy going.   When She would get peeved at Him, He would laugh it off.   One day She got out of humor waiting for Him when He was nearly an hour late.   "You make me so mad," She told Him, "sometimes I feel like shaking you."   "You're just in love with me, that's all;" He told Her.   "If you could just control your temper long enough to see it, you'd make the best little wife in the world."

138.   He went on a cross-country trip for His company, and had jokingly promised to be untrue to Her memory only if He could find a prettier girl.   When He got to Kansas City he wrote back: "Dearest: I couldn't find a single girl half as pretty

or as nice as you, and I've travelled 1700 miles. Why waste my time making me keep looking on the way back. Promise to marry me and I'll be in a daze all the way home."

139.   She got a job in a factory where He was the straw-boss. She soon learned to handle a machine saw, but one day, by mistake in calculation, cut off a bracket one inch short. "Are you going to fire me?" She asked Him tremulously. "No," He told Her, "I'm going to marry you and give you lessons at night, before you cut your nose off on that saw."

140.   He was a hardworking cynic. He hated everybody and everything. Then He met Her, and He went for Her the way coal goes into cellars. He loved her for years but he never proposed. He hated marriage. One day He realized She was fed up with being kept hanging that way, and He told Her: "I don't know if I'm right about debunking everything, or if I'm wrong. If I'm wrong, then marriage is all right too, and I ought to get married. If I'm right I ought to have a son to carry on my grudge after I'm dead. Let's get married."

141.   He had been with a scientific expedition in the Rio Tinto of Brazil, and had been lost two years and a prisoner of headhunters. "What did you think of all those nights, before you managed to escape?" She asked Him, when He had come home safe . "I kept thinking I'd never want to be a prisoner again as long as I lived," He told Her. "But when I got home and heard

you hadn't even had a date with another fellow while I was gone, I decided that I could stand being the prisoner of a girl like you for life."

142.   He was a lawyer and could face a savage jury or a scathing district attorney, but He couldn't get up the nerve to propose in person.   Finally He had a court recorder make Him a fancy scroll to send Her, saying: "You are charged with living in a state of single blessedness, much to the damage of the feelings and happiness of the undersigned, also known as the party of the second heart.   If found guilty you will be sentenced to be my lawful wife forever, darling."

143.   She was the only girl in a family with six brothers, and She had to do the washing because Her mother was an invalid. He was always kept waiting on their date-nights, while She finished the laundry.   Finally one night He said: "I thought when you got the washing machine I'd be able to have some time with you, but now that I see that even with a machine it takes all night to do the washing for a family of nine.   I think I'll marry you and have you wash for only two or maybe three; and your brothers can hire a maid for your mother."

144.   One night at a party He drew a forfeit that He had to kiss the prettiest girl in the room or the four bare legs of a chair. "I'll do better than that," He said, marching right up to Her and

giving Her an enormous kiss. "I'll ask Her to marry me right now."

145. They went for a ride in a rowboat and She stood up suddenly to wave to someone, and capsized the boat. When they had paddled ashore and were looking at their sopping clothes between laughter and tears, She said ruefully: "I guess I'd make a terrible sailor." "Yes," He agreed promptly, "but you'd make a wonderful mate."

146. He worked at the desk next to Hers in the office and was always remarking on the fellows He saw Her going out with. Finally one day she got sore, and said: "What do you care who I go out with? Do I tell you what girls to go out with?" "No," He admitted, "but you don't love me, and I love you. If you should ever begin to worry about what girl I go out with, tell me, will you, and I'll marry you so quick, the minister will need two people to help him marry us: one to say 'Here they come,' and another to say 'There they go'." Two months later they were married.

147. One night they were sitting admiring the moon, and She began describing the dream-home She had had in Her heart ever since She was little and read fairy-tale books. He listened all the way through, and then added: "In among all the ginger-bread cornices and hearthseats, would there be anywhere to tuck one quiet husband?"

148.   He kept complaining about Her going out with other men while She was supposed to be His girl. "You don't understand," She told Him. "One of these days the cat will let go of your tongue and you're going to propose, and I love you so I won't be able to refuse. Meanwhile I'm going out with other fellows till I get sick of them." That was more than a hint. He proposed.

149.   They were at a carnival and the silhouette man snagged them. "Just sit here a minute," he promised them, "I'll make a beautiful silhouette of the lady for only a quarter." When he was finished, he handed the bit of black cardboard over, saying, "Here you are, Mister, a lovely picture of your wife." "Not my wife," He told the silhouette-man, "my future wife—I hope."

150.   One afternoon at the zoo, She kept making a fuss over all the animal babies, the monkey babies, the elephant babies, the zebra babies, all of them. "If you like babies so much," He asked Her, "why don't you have a couple of your own?" "I want to very much," She said, "but I was sort of thinking of getting married first. That is, if you intend to ask me." After that, he didn't need to ask her. He knew her answer.

151.   She was an ardent baseball rooter and knew all the boys on the team, and she always got a seat just behind home-plate. He was the pitcher, but one of the team's worst batters, and he came up to bat when a single-bagger was all that was needed

to bring in three runs and clinch the game. "Hit that singleton and I'll kiss you," She shouted wildly. He turned and smiled and hit a homerun. When He came around to collect, He insisted that a homerun was worth four kisses. After collecting them He wiped off His mouth thoughtfully, while the spectators roared, and said: "Listen, if you'll marry me, and I can come home to kisses like that every night we'll win the pennant."

152.   She was an actress and getting to be well-known and She went under the name of Sidonie Addams. One night at a premiere someone addressed Her escort as "Mr. Addams." On the way home in a cab, He said: "You know, if I weren't afraid I'd be called Mr. Addams permanently, I'd marry you." "Darling," She told Him, "the day we get married I'll retire from the stage."

153.   She had made a bathing suit out of two bandana handkerchiefs, and asked him how he liked it. He looked both ways along the beach, and twice at her beautiful figure, before he answered. "I don't know whether to marry you because you're so economical with material," He said, "or whether to marry you so I can stand up for you in court when they arrest you for indecent exposure in that outfit. Either way, though, I'm going to marry you."

154.   He was coming home after a long absence, and he telegraphed on ahead to Her: "Will you marry me. Question

mark. When. Question mark. Where. Question mark."
When She met Him at the station, She didn't speak when He
kissed Her, but handed him a telegraph blank on which was
printed "Yes. Exclamation point. Anytime. Period. Anyplace.
Period."

155   She was trying to become an actress, but was very disappointed in the small parts She got. One day She complained
to Him that after two months of looking, all She found was a
part where She would be saying "The house is on fire" every
night at 9.22 P. M. "Don't worry," He told Her, "anytime you
get fed up with it, I have a nice part for you where every night
at 6.22 P.M. You say, 'Darling, dinner is ready!' "

156.   They were talking about their health, and She said:
"You know, men can never be as healthy as women, because
they have one rib less, the rib of Adam's that Eve was made
out of." "Sweetheart," He told Her, "that's only superstition,
but if you really believe it, maybe you'd better marry me, and
give me my rib back."

157.   They were having a Gay Nineties party, and She came
as an old-fashioned school-girl, with a bow in Her hair, a short
dress, and a slate with chalk hanging down on a string. During the party everyone began singing "School-Days" for Her,
and when they came to the line "When I wrote on your slate
'I love you so'," She held up the slate, and much to her sur-

prise, there were the words written on it. She looked at Him, and he smiled guiltily. "Turn it over," He said. She turned it over, and on the other side the message went on: ". . . .so will you marry me."

158. She was complaining about how men always wanted to get married. "Why look at all the trouble it is to be married," She said; "you have to cook, and mend, and blow the children's noses, and oh, a thousand things." "Yes," He agreed, "but look at what you don't have to do any more. You don't have to go to the office, or 'yes' the boss, or spend all your money on clothes and cosmetics because I'd be paying the bills." "Why you?" She asked. "You know darn well why," He insisted; "because I'm going to marry you if I have to tie you hand and foot to do it."

159. He sent her an interoffice memo, marked "Look out the window at 3.30." At 3.30 She looked out the window and there was a little note on a string from the window above, saying: "Look out the window again at 3.40." Ten minutes later there was a heart-shaped box of candy, with a note telling Her to look out again in ten more minutes. At 3.50 She rushed to the window and looked up, but nothing was hanging there. She heard a laugh and looked across the way, and there he was in the window opposite with a big red ribbon around his neck and a sign on him saying: "One Husband. Easy Terms. Take Advantage of This Unusual Bargain. Please."

160.   He took His girl to his mother's 25th wedding anniversary party.   When the cake was cut everyone insisted that His
mother make a speech, and He insisted loudest of All.   "All
right," she said, standing up; "all I have to say is that this is
the next-to-the-happiest day of my life."   "What's the happiest?"
everyone shouted.   "It's a toss-up," she admitted, "between the
day of my wedding, and the day my son will marrry the girl he
loves."   What was there for Him to do but propose?

161.   She slipped on an orange peel, and would have fallen
badly if He hadn't been there to catch Her.   "I hope you're
there the next time I fall on a peel," She said, gratefully.   "And
I hope the next peel you come across," He told Her. "is the peal
of wedding bells — ours."

162.   She was always saying She wouldn't get married "until
the right man came along," so one night when He came to
see Her, He walked in the front door, tipped his hat, and walked
out the back door without saying a word.   Then He went
around the lawn and came through again.   He made the trip
about six times before She finally stopped laughing long enough
to ask Him what it was all about.   "I was just hoping," He
explained, "that one of these times you'd mistake me for the
'right man coming along,' and marry me."

163.   "Would you ever join a Lonely-Hearts Club?" She asked
Him.   "Never," He assured Her.   "My heart is never going to

be lonely." "But how can you be sure?" She wanted to know. "Because I'm going to marry you," He told Her, "and love you for the rest of my life."

164.   She promised to marry Him as soon as She learned to cook, but months went by and She didn't seem to be learning very fast.   One night he came to see her with a little flat package.   "No, it's not a cook-book," He told Her.   "But I bought it in the restaurant at the corner.   Open it up and find out." She opened it, and in it was a little blue and silver sign saying: "If your wife can't cook, eat here, and keep her for a pet." "Well," He wanted to know.   "You don't know what a relief that is," She told Him; "because I couldn't ever learn to cook."

165.   He was the picture of health, and She couldn't understand it when He said they couldn't go out because He had spent all his money on the doctor. That happened several times, and She became worried. "What's the matter with you?" She wanted to know, "is it your heart?" "It's my heart all right," He told Her "I love you so much, I'm getting palpitations, and I don't think the doctor can cure me.   How about marrying me and nursing me back to health?   I saved enough, by us not going out the last three times, to make a down payment on the ring."

166.   They were on Main Street and saw a little store where newspapers could be bought with any headline you like printed

on it. He asked her to wait, and went in, and a few minutes later He came out with a newspaper and stood on the corner hollering "Extra, Extra, Read all about it," until She was afraid He would be arrested. "I'll buy your paper," She told Him. "Not for sale, lady," He told Her, "this paper is for the girl I love." And He flashed the headline: NAME THE DAY, DARLING, SAYS HOPELESS LOVER.

167.   At an amusement park they wanted to go in the Tunnel of Love. "If you're married," the barker told them, "you can both go for the price of one." "Does it count if we're just engaged?" He asked. "Sure," said the barker. "What do you say, sweetheart?" He asked Her. "Two can live as cheaply as one, can't they?"

168.   She was a country girl, and He worked for the milk company. One day while waiting for the driver to weigh the milk, He went with Her to gather newly laid eggs. He had been coming around a long time, and She let Him kiss Her on the way back. Somehow the basket of eggs slipped and all the eggs were broken. "You won't tell, will you?" She asked. "I don't know," He said pretending to be very serious. "Better marry me and make sure. After all, a husband can't be made to testify against his wife."

169.   They had been playing bridge with friends and had won, and as He took Her home, She said: "You're pretty lucky at

cards, aren't you?   You held some wonderful hands tonight."
"Darling," He told Her, taking Her hands in His, "these are the
only two hands I want to hold every night for the rest of my
life."

170.   She worked in the offices of a political party, and was
getting on well. He wasn't sure She really wanted to get married and give up Her job, so He was backward about proposing.
One night at the movies, the heroine made the remark: "Any
woman would give up the finest career in the world for her own
man, her own home, and her own children."   "Is that the truth,
darling?" He whispered. "Of course it is," she whispered
back; "but is this a proposal?"   "Positively," He said.

171.   He was very homely, and it preyed on His mind.   "I'd
ask you to marry me," He told Her one night, "but I have a face
that only a mother could love."   "Well you go ahead and ask
me to marry you," She encouraged Him, "and before we're
married very long maybe I'll *be* a mother."

172.   She had told Him, and only half in jest, that She intended to marry a man with a million dollars.   One evening She
noticed that every time He kissed Her, He marked it down
in a little book.   "What are you doing," She asked, "keeping
score?"   "No," He replied, "but each of your kisses is worth a
thousand dollars to me.   I have only nine-hundred and ninety-

three kisses to go before I'm a millionaire, and can propose.

173.   "You know," He told Her; "I made a terrible mistake at
the shop this morning, and the foreman said to me: 'If you go
on that way, son, you'll never be the head of the business.   You
better get married and at least be the head of a family.'"
"Well?" She asked.   "Well," He went on, "I was thinking of
taking his advice; how about it?"

174.   She was very tiny and very cute, and consequently very
vain.   You could get almost anything from Her by appealing
to Her vanity, and He knew it.   One night He began flattering
her hair-do, praising the smallness of her feet, enthusing about
her ears, and down through the whole list until She was fairly
purring.   "There's only one thing wrong with you," He finished.
She sat up fast.   "What's wrong with me?" She wanted to
know.   "Well," He explained, "you're everything in the world
a girl can be except some man's wife.   Do you suppose it would
be fun being my wife?"   She supposed.

175.   She knew He walked in His sleep, so one evening when
She walked into the parlor where He was dozing while waiting
for Her to finish bathing and dressing for their date, She wasn't
surprised when He walked up to Her with his arms outstretched
and His eyes shut and said: "Darling, I'm mad about you.   If
you won't marry me, I'll do something terrible!"   Thinking He
was asleep and should not be crossed, She said: "Yes, yes, I'll

marry you." Before She knew it He had His arms around Her
and opened one eye in a broad wink. "That's all I want to hear
you say for the next hour," He said.

176.   He had never seen Her before they met at a party where
they were playing a game of Truth or Consequences. The question was: "Have you ever met your dream-girl?" and when it
came His turn to answer He said boldly, "I certainly have. Tonight. And there she is," He continued, pointing right at Her.
"I think he's fibbing," She said, blushing. "Why we're perfect
strangers." "All right," He said, "If I'm fibbing make the 'con-
sequence' that I have to marry you and prove you are my dream
girl." Four months later the proposal got to the church-bells
stage.

177.   He was a radio trouble-shooter, and had to go to Chicago
in a hurry, so He was going to take the plane. She didn't want
Him to. She was afraid of airplanes, and He couldn't talk her
out of it. "No, no, no," She insisted, "I don't care if they fire
you if you get there a day late. I'd rather have a live husband
out of work than a dead boy-friend in a coffin." "Are you proposing to me?" He laughed. "I'd better," She said. "This may
be my last chance if that plane crashes."

178.   "Do you think that when a man tells a girl he loves her
he ought to marry her?" She asked, referring to Her younger
sister's problems. "I don't know about men in general," He

said, "but when I love a girl, I want to marry her all right."
"Anybody I know?" She asked airily, trying not to hear Her
heart thump. "You know darn well it's you I love," He said;
"and you I'm going to marry."

179.   They were discussing occultism. "If you believe in
thought transmission," He challenged Her, "see if you can read
my mind. I'm concentrating." There was a long silence, and
She looked undecided. "Can't you get the message?" He laughed.
"Oh, I get the message all right," She said, "but one of the
words is hazy. It's either 'proposal' or 'proposition'." He smiled
and kissed Her. "It's 'proposal', honey," He assured Her.

180.   They were on a bus together, and were so lost in spoon-
ing that they passed their stop and didn't realize where they
were till the conductor called: "All out! End of the line. City
Hall." They looked at each other with smiles. "What do you
say, sweetheart," He asked; "we got here in a daze; shall we
wander in and get married the same way?" "I'm willing," She
agreed, "But I'm not in any daze. I knew the bus stopped here
all the time."

181.   She was a very ardent supporter of woman's rights. "I'll
never get married," She told Him one day when Her whole
family was around. "Why don't you go and get yourself another girl? I can hold my own against any man. Why should I
get married?" Instead of answering He stood up and picked

Her up bodily and held Her up in the air over His head in spite of Her screaming and kicking. "So you can hold your own against any man?" He panted, while her family laughed themselves sick. "Well you're going to stay up there until you say either 'Uncle' or 'I'll marry you'." She didn't say 'Uncle.' It's funny how brute strength appeals to these strong-minded girls more than to the feminine ones.

182. He was going away for a while, but he promised to call Her long distance. "I've never made any bones about how much I love you," She told Him. "I'll wait by the telephone every night for your ring." "Not 'for' my ring, darling," He said; " 'with' it." And he slipped an engagement ring on her finger.

183. He was very fond of his dog, but He had to leave it behind when He took a job on a ship. "I'd like to have your dog," She told Him, "if you don't want to give him to strangers." "Not only to strangers," He said, "but only to a relative. The only way you'll get that dog is if you marry me, and keep him in the family." "Yes," She told Him, "I will. And maybe we could even have a baby to keep the dog company."

184. They were coming home from the movies, and stopped under a tree in the darkest part of the street while He kissed Her again and again. She loved it. "Oh darling," She sighed, "I wish we could go on kissing forever." "Well," He said, practi-

cally, "we'd have to stop to eat once in a while; but if you marry me we'll have real long stretches of it without interruption."

185.   It was the night of graduation, and they were watching the June moon together.   "I wonder how much it will cost to have our diplomas framed," She asked suddenly.   "I don't know," He admitted, "but I know a way to cut the cost in half. We write 'Mr. & Mrs.' before the name on mine, and just have that one framed."

186.   She was collecting some old clothes from her friends, for distribution with baskets of food to poor people on Thanksgiving. When She asked Him for something, He hastily checked over in His mind what He could do without in his wardrobe.   "How would you like some old shoes?" He asked. "Thrown at me, darling," She replied, as quick as a flash.   But He always insisted that He had done the proposing.

187.   "You know what?" He asked Her.   "No," She said, "What?" "I dreamed that I proposed to you," He told Her. "That's been my dream too," She murmured; "but tell me, did I accept?" "I don't know," He admitted, "I got so flustered I woke up." "Well you go back to sleep," She advised Him, "and see what I say.   But I warn you, if the girl in the dream says 'no,' you're dreaming of somebody else, not me."

188.   She was a nurse and He had appendicitis.   When the

doctor dressed his incision, it hurt very much, but after the doctor was through She would put a dressing on that felt very soft and soothing. "You know," He told Her one morning; "in the three weeks I've been on my back here, I've gotten to know your step and to wait for it. And that dressing every day is my idea of Heaven. If it's true that the way to a man's heart is through his stomach, you've sure made the trip. Will you marry me when I get out of here?" "You ask me again then," She laughed. "I think you're delirious." But he wasn't, and he asked her again, and she accepted too.

189.   She was a waitress in a soda-fountain, and She rather liked Him because His underfed look brought out the mother in Her. One evening He noticed her slipping an egg into His malted milk on the sly. She was very embarrassed when He asked Her about it, and tried to kid her way out of it. "It'll make you strong," She told Him. "How can you kiss your girl if you aren't strong?" "I haven't got a girl," He told Her, "and I don't want one. But I do want a wife, and something tells me that you're the wife for me."

190.   She worked evenings as an usherette, and He worked mornings as a milkman. In between they both slept. After trying vainly for weeks to sandwich in some time to see Her between their jobs, He said: "I can't stand the hours, honey. Either we get married and see each other afternoons, or we break up." "Is that a proposal or a threat?" She wanted to

know.   "Well," He suggested, "let's kiss and see if we feel
more like getting into a wedding or an argument."

191.   He didn't have much faith in Himself, and could never
quite get around to proposing.   When He was going on his
vacation, He said to Her: "You know, I get three weeks this
year, not two.   It would make a wonderful honeymoon, if
you'd marry me, but I guess you won't."   "Who said I
wouldn't?" She countered.   "I will if you get up a little faith
in yourself, and ask me."

192.   She moved to Texas, and kept writing back to Him
how wonderful the people out there are.   "If I moved out
there," He wrote back, "how long would I have to live there
before I could call myself a Texan, and be wonderful enough
for you to marry?"

193.   They were in Washington, helping each other look for
rooms.   The clerk at the renting agency handed them one
card that described a nice two-room apartment with kitchenette
"suitable for two girls or a young married couple."   "If you
were only a girl," She laughed, "our problem would be settled."
"I'd rather stay a man," He told Her, "and settle the problem
by marrying you."

194.   It was Thanksgiving and He had been invited to Her
house.   Her father had a custom of asking everyone what they

were thankful for before giving them their helping of turkey. When it came His turn he said "I'm thankful that I finally got up enough courage just now to make this a proposal of marriage."

195.   He was a lifeguard at a lake, and was not allowed to spend His time talking to the swimmers. She went out in a canoe and tipped it over purposely so He would have to swim out to Her. After doing this two or three times in one afternoon, He said: "You know it's lots of fun swimming out and kissing you in the water, but somebody might really be drowning meanwhile. Let's get married and do our kissing at home."

196.   They were on a boatride up the Hudson on a very hot summer day. "Oh my," She complained, fanning herself with her handkerchief. "It's just too hot to do anything but sit." "Or sit and think," He added. "No," She insisted, "just sit." "Well," He inquired, "would it be easier to think too if what you were thinking about was whether to say yes or no to a proposal of mariage?" "I guess it would," She laughed; "why, am I getting one?" "I don't know for sure," He teased Her; "maybe it's too hot to propose. . . ." But it wasn't too hot to seal the bargain with a kiss.

197.   They went to kindergarten together, also to public school, and high-school. Then they went to college together.

When graduation was coming up, He asked Her if She were going to take a post-graduate course, and when She said She was, He said He was too. "You know, He added, "after all these years of going to school together we probably have more in common with each other than with anyone else in the world. Maybe we ought to get married." "Well, it's about time," She sighed. "It's taken you seventeen years to get educated enough to phrase a proposal. And all I'm educated enough to do is to say 'yes'."

198. His father had died when he was about eleven, and He had gone to work after school then, and by fourteen was working full time. Consequently life was a pretty serious business to Him. She was full of fun and liveliness, as pert and volatile as a sunbeam. "You're the exact opposite of me, "He told Her finally, "so I guess it must be true that opposites attract. I'm very much in love with you, and if you married me I might see the enjoyable side of things more often." "And maybe you'd show me how to see the serious side once in a while," She agreed. "We'll make a wonderful pair."

199. He was shy about proposing, so He put an ad in the agony column of the newspaper saying: "If a certain beautiful girl named L. D. ever sees this, it's just to let her know that a certain dumb bunny named F. R. gets tongue-tied every time he tries to propose." Friends showed it to Her and She put an

ed in the next day, saying: "If a certain dumb bunny named
F. R. ever sees this, it's just to let him know that L. D. is ready,
willing, and able."

200.   "It's a funny thing," He told Her one night. "Here we
are in New York.   There are seven million people in this town.
Three and a half million are women.   Of them, one third are
married, and one third have boy friends already, that leaves
about one million.   Of them, one third are too old and one
third are too young, then of the right ones, one third are too
fat and one third are too thin, and of the ones that are left, one
third are too blonde and one third are too brunette, and of the
two that are left in the end, one is my sister and the other one
is you. Will you marry me?"

201.   They were sitting in the park when an airplane came by
overhead. She remarked on how glamorous a pilot's life must
be. "Well, glamor is as glamor does," He told Her; "purse
your lips, gorgeous, because I'm coming in on the beam, and
we'll make a happy landing in matrimony. Better say yes, or
there'll be stormy weather."

202.   She took Him to visit some married friends, hoping to
nudge Him into the proposal He had been very backward about
getting around to.   But to Her horror, all Her married friends
did during the visit was to fight and throw things. On the way
home She did not dare bring up the subject of marriage, but

He did. "Darling," He said, "I haven't proposed to you for a reason. I always felt married life would be pretty dull. Now I know it won't be. Let's buy all breakable furniture, light enough for throwing, and get married."

203.   They were victims of puppy-love, both being only about twelve. "Ten years from now I'm going to call on you and ask you something," He promised Her mysteriously. Naturally She forgot all about it, but He had written it down, and He turned up one day and reminded Her of it. "And what's the question?" She smiled. "Now that I see what a gorgeous girl you turned out to be," He told Her gallantly, "the question is: How about marrying me?"

204.   He was quite a bit older than She was, and was taking a lot of kidding from His friends on being a "cradle-robber." One night She refused Him a date, and He stayed up all night feeling jealous, sure She was taking up with some younger fellow. The next night He came over unexpectedly and said: "Sweetheart, I can't stand the idea of losing you to some other man. Let's get married." She smiled. "I didn't have a date last night," She admitted. "I just wanted to know if you cared enough to worry about it."

205.   He was shy about proposing but He wanted to marry Her in the worst way. One day at the races He said to Her: "There's a horse named 'Marriage' running in the fifth race. I

put my roll on his nose, and if he comes in I'm going to marry you." "Quick," She laughed, "put my bet on him too." The horse lost, but they got married anyhow.

206.   He was a patient in the hospital, and very hard to get along with.   She was a nurse and put up with His temper, and handled Him perfectly all through His illness.   A week after He left, He was back with an enormous bouquet for her and tickets to the best show in town.   After the show, riding back to the hospital in a cab, He said: "You're a wonderful nurse, I only realize it now.   I'll bet you'd make a wonderful wife." "It's a bet," She said; "but what happens if I lose?"   "Then I smother you with kisses," He told Her.

207.   Her last name began with an O, but in having some matched luggage stamped, a mistake was made and they stamped the whole set Q.   She was heartbroken, and told Him so.   "Easiest thing in the world," He told Her.   "My last name begins with a Q.   Marry me."

208.   He called Her up on April 1st.   "Darling," He said, "I have to leave town on my job, and I want you to marry me and come along."   "Quit your kidding," She said.   "I know it's April Fool's Day.   "Maybe it is," He said, "but I'm not fooling."   "All right," She agreed, "but if I get left waiting at the Church, the joke will be on me."   He was there in ten minutes with a ring, and then She believed Him.

209.   She was a dentist's assistant, and He was just a man with a toothache.   He looked at Her, and all his pain was gone, so He left the office.   This happened about three times, and the third time the dentist wanted to know what was going on. When He told the dentist, the girl said, "Be careful, you'll get me fired."   "That's what I'm hoping," He came back; "then I can marry you."

210.   She was walking into the post-office when a tall young man came up and said: "Will you marry me; I love you?"   He was a perfect stranger and She began to be worried until She saw about six boys with college sweaters standing nearby with paddles watching Him.   So She fell in with the joke and said, "Oh sure."   A few weeks later they met by accident at a basket-ball game.   They made a date, then another, and finally one night He said, "Darling, there's nobody standing behind me with a paddle making me say it this time.   I love you, will you marry me?"

211.   She had gone with Him a long time and He never proposed.   One day She told him She was going to get married before she was twenty-five if She had to marry the first man that She met on the street.   He still didn't ask, and went home quietly.   About an hour later She was going out to the drugstore and he jumped out from behind a hedge, and said: "I'm the first man you met on the street.   You've got to marry me."

"You big ninny," She said; "I'm dying to, but you don't need to scare me into a fit, do you?"

212.   She had roomed with another girl all the way through college, and when She came to the big city, She told Him it was lonesome living alone. "Want me to live with you?" He asked, half in a joke. "Sure," She admitted, "but the landlady would worry unless we were married." Thus the bells rang and they soon were joined in wedlock.

213.   She loved flowers, but She lived in an apartment. He lived in a big house left Him by His father. "You don't know how I envy you all that space you have for growing flowers," She told Him. "Well, as my wife all that space would be yours," He said. And it was so.

214.   She was a governess and He was a friend of the family. He got to like Her and wrote to Her often. One day while visiting the house, one of the children that She took care of kept staring at Him, and when He asked why, the child said: "Oh, I'm waiting to see you kiss Miss Dwight." "What makes you think I'm going to?" He asked. "Oh, because she loves you," the child explained artlessly; "She always cries when she gets a letter from you." He turned to Her questioningly; Her eyes were cast down in confession. "I don't see why," He said to the child, "Anytime She wants to marry me and stop

crying, I'll be the happiest man in the world, and I'll bet I'll cry too."

215.   He was a bandleader and was preparing to go on tour. "I wish I were a singer," She told Him, "so I could go along too." "You can come along without being able to sing a note," He assured Her, "we have just the opening for you—my wife."

216.   He called Her up long-distance to propose, but then He got tongue-tide. Before He could spill out the fateful question, the lady-operator butted in with "Your time is up, Sir." "For Heaven's sake," He begged the operator, "have a heart, I'm trying to propose, but I don't have the thirty cents for another five minutes. Do you think she'll marry me anyhow?" "Sorry," giggled the operator, "but I do not have that information, Sir. Take another five minutes and ask her yourself."

217.   He had a nice voice and so did She. At parties they were always being called on to sing duets. One day they were even asked to perform in "Oh Promise Me" at a wedding. They sang it in alternate verses and then in harmony. When they watched the bride and groom kiss, He could not stand it any more. "Let's make a permanent thing out of our duet," He said, "and make life one sweet song together." "Maybe even a trio?" She suggested shyly.

218.   "Which would you rather have," He asked Her unex-

pectedly one night, "a new hat or a new coat, if you needed
both." "Why, a new coat," She said surprised. "And which
new shoes or a permanent wave?" "A permanent, of course,"
She said. "Now what's all this about?" "Oh nothing," He
smiled, "I just wanted to see whether you were practical or vain.
I guess you're a little of both. That makes just the right combination, it seems— to me. If I make the right combination for
you, will you marry me?" "We combine," She agreed. Sealed
with a kiss.

219. He had been in a terrible accident and came through
without a scratch. "Were you scared?" She wanted to know.
"I sure was," He said, "I thought I was going to be killed without ever having had you for my own wife. And I'm twice as
scared now, trying to get up the nerve to ask you to marry me."

220. He loved Her and told Her so, but She said She didn't
want to marry a man just for a meal-ticket. She wanted to prove
She could make Her own living for a while. She got a job and
made good, and before the year was up was earning more than
He was. "I can't ask you to marry me now," He told Her.
"You earn more than I do." "Don't let that stop you," She told
Him, "I'm saving my money. I won't be earning it long. I'd
rather have a husband than a job."

221. They were at her sister's house, and He picked up the
pride and joy of the household, a son about a year old,

and put it in Her arms before a mirror and stood next to Her. "Don't we make a nice family group?" He asked. "Yes," She agreed, "but it looks like a little unconventional without a ring here." And She held up the third finger of Her left hand. "I can fix that," He assured Her, and swiftly took out an engagement ring and put it on her hand.

222. They were having a candy-party in Her apartment, and She had cleaned everything specially and waxed the kitchenette floor till it shone like a mirror. Then, carrying out the candy to the guests, She slipped and fell with a crash on the linoleum floor. He rushed over to pick Her up. "Promise me you'll never wax our floors," He whispered, "and I'll pick you up and carry you right to a church." So it ended up as an engagement party.

223. He had never kissed a girl in His life. "I love you terribly," He admitted to Her one night, "and I want to marry you the worst way, but I've never even kissed a girl, and I'm not sure I ought to get married until I've had some experience." "I've never been kissed, either," She told him, "you go ahead and propose, and we'll get our experience together." They got married and lived happily ever after.

224. She was interested in interior decoration, and moved all the furniture in the house around until Her parents were wild. "Listen," He told Her one night; "you can pick between a home

and a career right now. I want to propose, but I don't dare so long as I don't know whether you wouldn't be wanting to shift all the furniture on our wedding night." "Not until the honeymoon was over at least," She laughed. "Good," He said, "because I don't intend for the honeymoon to ever be over."

225.   He'd been trying to propose for months, but lacked the nerve. Finally he bought a parrot and taught it to say: "Alice, Joe loves you. Why don't you marry him?" Then He invited Her over and and was out when She arrived. When He got back She said, "I've been having the most interesting conversation with your parrot." "And what have you decided?" He asked. "Well, I couldn't disappoint a nice friendly bird like that," She laughed. And the parrot let out a loud whistle as they kissed.

226.   He won a telephone call on a radio quizz program. So He called Her up. "Listen darling," He said, "there are three hundred people right here that I can see listening in, and about a million over the air. I want them all to know. I love you like crazy. Will you marry me now, or should I keep on broadcasting?" "Yes, I'll marry you, you imbecile," She said; "only hang up now and come and ask me in person. I'm not sure it's legal this way."

227.   She had a reputation for being fickle, and had been engaged several times, only to break the engagements off. He

fell for Her like a ton of bricks anyway, and one night He told
Her: "They say you're fickle and always break off engagements,
so I won't propose and take a chance. If you think I'll make a
good husband, come on right now down to the Church and
let's get married. The minister is waiting." She agreed, but She
asked: "Didn't you take a big chance that I might say no?"
"Sure," said He, "but it was a bigger chance I'd be taking if I
proposed and gave you a chance to get bored with me before
we were married."

228.   She was always saying that anyone who got married with
the world in the state it's in was a fool. During the year they
went around together, two of their best friends got married, and
two others got engaged. "Seems like everybody is just a fool,"
He told her one night. "What's the use being sane, though,
when everybody else is crazy? Let's us get married too."

229.   He was a musician. She was stubborn. For a long time
he could not get her to say, "Yes." One day he decided to
woo her with music. He would play one romantic tune after
another until she'd say, "Yes." So he played first "I'll be Loving
You Always," "A Little Love, a Little Kiss," "A Bicycle Built
for Two," "You're the Only One" and so on. Time wore on.
He looked at the clock and played "It's Three O'clock in the
Morning." She began to nod. He hurried with "Oh Promise
Me." She really nodded. He ended with Mendelssohn's
"Wedding March."

230.   "Will you invite me to your wedding?" He asked Her
suddenly. "But I'm not even engaged," She said, surprised.
"Oh, I forgot to mention it," He said, "I meant, will you invite
me as the groom?"

231.   He wrote Her a letter written in a circle, reading: "If
you love me and I love you why don't we get married If you
love me &c. . . . " She wrote back in the same kind of circle:
"Certainly I love you if you love me so let's get married because
certainly I love you &c. . . ."

232.   He was telling Her about a dream He had. "There
were dozens of diamond rings floating through the air," He said.
"You should have caught one," She laughed. "I did," He said,
pulling one out of his picket, "And strangely enough it has
your initials and mine inside."

233.   They were ice-skating, and He kept edging closer and
closer to a dangerous hole in the ice carefully marked with a
big sign. "What's the matter," She said finally, "can't you see
that big Danger sign?" "No," He told Her, "I'm blind-drunk
on love; and I won't be able to see another thing till you promise
to marry me." "All right, I promise," She said.

234.   Someone gave Him a Bible to wear next to his heart
when He went hunting, to stop a possible bullet. He told Her
about it, and added: "How about giving me a picture of you

to wear there instead, so if I get killed it will be with you next to my heart." "If you love me so much, why do you go hunting, when it's so dangerous?" She wanted to know. "Aha," He cried, "reforming me already, and we aren't even married yet." "Are we getting married?" She asked coyly. "Just as soon as you name the day," He told Her.

235. She was very plain, but He loved Her anyhow, as She was very sweet and honest and beautifully built. "What would you say, if I told you I loved you?" He asked Her one afternoon. "I'd say you were crazy," She told His frankly; "When there are so many prettier girls around." "Well then I'm crazy," He said, "because I think you're the sweetest, finest, most honest girl I ever met, and you'll still be sweet and fine when all those pretty girls are nasty ugly old women. Please be my wife."

236. They had a fight and She told Him to leave Her apartment and never come back. "Can I take something for a souvenir?" He asked angrily. "Anything you like," She answered, just as angrily. So he picked Her up in his arms and started carrying Her out. She began to struggle but He wouldn't put Her down. "Even when we fight, you're the only girl for me," He told Her. "Let's get married and do our fighting regularly."

237. He was a welder and had taken several months learning,

but He was sure of a good job when He finished the course. When the day came and He got the job, He rushed over to Her, and told Her the good news. "And do you know what my first assignment is?" He asked Her. "No, what?" "Welding your life to mine, now that I can earn a good living." And that's how it was.

238.   She was in love with the football team coach at high school, but didn't know how to tell Him, so She took to hanging around the team at practice, and they made Her their mascot at games. When the end of the season came, and She was going to graduate, the boys on the team insisted they were going to have Her around next year. "But you can't," She told them, "I'm going to college." "Oh no, you're not," they said, "you're going to marry Coach Fitz and stay here." "But he's never asked me," She objected. "He will," they promised her, and they went and got Him, and piled on Him in a football scrimmage and swore they wouldn't get off till he proposed. He did.

239.   He was always arguing with Her, and one night they were parked on a dark street and arguing loudly. Someone stuck his head out of a window and hollered: "Why don't you two hire a hall and argue there?" "I have a better idea," He told Her, "let's hire a home and argue in private before we get arrested for disturbing the peace." "But we'd get arrested for that too unless we were married," She objected. "Well then," He agreed, "we could get married too."

240. He came over specifically to propose one night, but He couldn't manage to get it out. She was all dressed up in expectation, as He had told Her to be prepared for a big surprise, but nothing happened. As She got up to see Him to the door when the time came to leave, Her earrings fell to the floor. They both got down on their knees to look for them, accidentally brushed together and kissed. "If we get married," He said, "we won't have to crawl around on the floor to kiss each other."

241. She was very fond of His mother, being an orphan Herself, and was always telling Him so. Finally He asked Her: "Would you be willing to accept her as your mother, with a little brother thrown in?" "No," She laughed; "I don't like little boys." "Well then, better marry me," He advised; "then you'll have to like me, and you'll get Mother as a premium."

242. They were sleighing and She slipped while pulling Her sled up the hill, and began slipping down on the hard-packed snow. Finally She fell and was skidding downhill rather fast, right into His way. He stopped Her by throwing Himself on the snow before Her. "Now I've caught you!" He cried gleefully, "And you'll have to marry me." "I might as well," She agreed; "I've obviously fallen for you."

243. He was at camp and She sent Him a cake. A letter came back by return mail: "Darling: I didn't get to eat much of your cake. All the other fellow ate it up, and they all say that

if I don't marry a girl that can cook like that I'm crazy. Will
you marry me? Even if it doesn't turn out right, I'll get to eat
some of your cake."

244.   They were coming home on the street-car, and He
stepped down first to help Her. Right at the car-stop was an
enormous puddle in which He had stepped squarely by so doing.
"How am I going to get over the water," She asked worriedly.
"Well," He said, "I could pick you up and lift you over, but
wouldn't that be awfully intimate unless we were engaged to
be married?" "It could be arranged," She told him demurely.

245.   She got a job as secretary-housekeeper to a young doctor
who had been living with His sister, who had died. One day his
schedule was particularly full, and while feeding Him lunch
She was prompting Him in all the different appointments He
had in the afternoon. "You aren't listening," She suddenly
noticed. "No," He admitted, "I was just wondering what I'd
do if you went and got married." "I guess you'd just have to
get another secretary," She guessed. "Not if I were the man
you went and married!" He pointed out.

246.   She was very proud to have learned the deaf-and-dumb
signal language in Her work, and wanted him to learn it too.
One evening He came around, and made primitive signs all
through supper, till Her whole family was in hysterics, but He
wouldn't say a word. Then, in the parlor with Her later, He

pointed to Her, to Himself, and to Heaven, then made signs like a minister, like a big kiss, and like rocking a baby in His arms. "You get the idea?" He finally asked. She nodded assent. "I'm speechless," She assured Him, lifting Her mouth for a kiss.

247. "Which would you rather marry," He asked Her, "a doctor or a lawyer?" "A doctor," She said. "I knew it," He exclaimed, "you're planning to get married!" And before She could remonstrate, He went on, "I better marry you before some quack or some shyster beats me to it!"

248. They had been going together for two years, and their hobby was going around looking at model homes for sale, although neither of them had ever mentioned marriage. One day She was raving about a particularly lovely home they had seen and He looked at Her searchingly and confessed: "Darling, I just paid a month's rent in advance on that little house." "But whatever for? It's much too big for just you," She said. "I thought maybe you'd help me fill it," He suggested.

249. She liked her boss very much, but one day, owing to the machinations of a crooked partner, He went broke. He called Her into His office. "Miss Martin," He said, "take a letter. 'Dear Miss Martin: I am broke, busted, flat on my aspirations, and out of business. I will have another business someday though, and as I can never hope to find another helper like you,

I want to marry you and keep you around till then. Please answer immediately.'" "The answer to that comes special delivery," She told Him, and came over and sat on His lap.

250.   They were sitting on the sofa, and He intended to propose without words by pulling out the ring and flashing it. But as He did so it fell between the sofa cushions, and the more they dug for it, the farther it disappeared. Finally it was gone from sight. "Well," He said morosely, "I guess I can't marry you now." "Oh you don't get away that easy," She assured Him, "If necessary, I'll carry this darn sofa down to the license bureau on my head."

251.   He went away on a long trip without proposing, although she had sincerely hoped He would. Her friends advised Her to write to Him saying She was considering getting married, by way of bringing Him to tow. She did, with some misgivings, and immediately He wrote very anxiously to know whom She was intending to marry. Forgetting all her friends' advice about making Him jealous, She took a chance and wrote back: "You, if you'll only ask me." He did.

252.   They were bathing and She couldn't swim, but She took a chance with an inflated tire and went out far over her head. Suddenly the tire began to hiss and deflate. She began calling for Him, and He swam out powerfully and began circling as She sank. "Why don't you save me, you idiot?" She cried. "I'm

just waiting for you to get desperate," He told Her; "so promise to marry me if I take you in." "I'm desperate." She said; "desperately in love." They both nearly drowned, trying to kiss in the water.

253. She was bragging how nothing could frighten Her. "I wish I were like that," He said. "I want to marry you the worst way, but every time I go to propose I get so scared my tongue gets paralyzed." "The only cure for that is marriage," She assured him solemnly.

254. He was an airplane pilot, and was always talking about airplanes. Finally She asked Him to take Her up. "Positively not," He said. "You're a jinx on planes. When I saw you the first time I went into a spin and a barrel-roll that I'm not out of yet. Do you think marrying you would straighten me out?"

255. They were at the movies, and She noticed He was whispering out the side of His mouth. "If you keep flirting with the girl next to you, you'll probably get arrested," She told Him. "I'm not flirting," He said. "I'm only practicing how to propose to you when the show is over." "Well for God's sake don't wait," said the man behind them very loudly. "Propose now and get it off your chest, so I can hear the show!"

256. "Funny isn't it?" He told Her one night. "A friend of mine is getting married, and he's so blind-drunk on love that

He kept falling over things and bumping into things all day."
"You'd never lose your head over a girl that way, would you?"
She asked hopelessly. He turned to look at Her when He heard
her unhappy inflection. "Never," He assured Her, and walked
directly into a telegraph pole. He sat down abruptly and began
to laugh. "It's a judgment," He said. "I guess I must be in
love. Shall we get married and find out?"

257.   She got a series of letters from him like this: "See your
doctor and have your heart checked up on." "Prepare for a
big shock." "Get a soft rug to faint on." "Big surprise coming
up." "Are you ready?" "Any minute now." "Hold the line."
"Here it comes!" "Will." "You." "Please . . ." "Sender
collapsed at this point. Message continued soon." "Will you
marry me, darling?"

258.   They were sitting together on the porch one afternoon
when Her father came home from skeet-shooting with an enormous shotgun in his hand. She looked at Him, and He looked
at Her, and they went off into gales of laughter. "It's all right,
Mr. Smith," He said, "I was just getting ready to propose anyhow."

259.   He was in the candle business, and one day He brought
around a package to show Her. In it were two small but mag-
nificent hand-ornamented candles. "These go on wedding
cakes," He told Her, "and we had a customer in today that

wanted to buy them. I was sort of saving them for my own wedding, and I didn't think I ought to sell them." "Your wedding?" She asked; "are you thinking of getting married? Anybody I know?" "I should say you know her," He said. "It's you!"

260.   He telephoned on Mother's Day and asked to speak to Her mother. When she got on the phone He said, "Do you suppose you could put up with an extra son for the next fifty or sixty years?" "I don't know," Her mother laughed; "I prefer to start with children when they're very small." "Well put Janet back on the phone," He said, "and maybe, if I can get up enough nerve to propose to Her, we can arrange it for a couple of small grandchildren for you." "Janet is listening in on the extension," Her mother said.

261.   He was at dinner at Her house when a fuse blew out. Her father and brother went down the cellar to fix it, and He took the opportunity to lean over and hug and kiss her in the dark. Suddenly the lights came on, and they were so engrossed in kissing, and with their eyes shut, that for a moment they didn't know everybody was looking at them, until they heard a roar of laughter. "I guess I've compromised you," He said. "If I marry you, will that make it all right?" "Yes!" everybody shouted. But just then Her small brother walked in and asked: "Should I unscrew the fuse again, Pop, or did he propose?"

262.   He took Her out, sat in the park with Her and watched the moon for a while. "Do you think looking at the moon makes people crazy?" He asked. "I suppose so," She said. "That's why they call them lunatics, isn't it?" "I guess so," He agreed, "because I'm certainly crazy about you. Will you marry me and nurse me back to sanity?" "I'll marry you," She said, "but I like your way of being crazy."

263.   They were walking down the street and they passed a bakery. The delicious aroma of new pastry, still hot, came wafting out, and He stopped with an inspired expression. "If you could only bake like that, I'd marry you," He assured Her grandly. "Let's go," She laughed, "baking is my specialty."

264.   He lived on a farm and had to go to Chicago. "I've got two cows and sixty-four chickens," He told Her, "and nobody to leave them with while I'm gone. I was going to ask you to take care of them, but that's an awful imposition on just a friend. Let's get married, and then I'll just be imposing on a relative." "Do you love me too," She asked, "or is this just for the sake of your livestock?" "Who do you suppose I want to go to Chicago and make lots of money for," he countered, "you or my chickens?"

265.   They were crossing the street one rainy day and she started to cross in front of a bus that had stopped at the corner. A car came whizzing out from behind it, and He snatched

Her back just in the nick of time. "I saved your life," He told Her roughly. "Now how about marrying me and saving mine, because if you don't I'll kill myself."

266.   She lived in a high building, and the elevator broke one day. She called Him up and told Him She was starving up on the thirtieth floor, and they wouldn't bring Her anything up to eat, and She didn't want to come down because how would She get up again to sleep. An hour later the bell rang, and there He was, panting from the long climb, and with a basket full of a hot dinner. "Oh, how can I ever thank you?" She asked. "By marrying me and living in a one-story cottage with me so this can never happen again," He said.

267.   "You know I don't believe in marriage," He told Her. "Yes," She said, a little dubiously. "I want to be a bachelor all my life," He went on, "but it might embarrass our children. Let's get married."

268.   She was always gushing about uniforms, and how romantic they made Her feel, so one day He showed up in a mailman's uniform. "Not that kind of a uniform, silly," She told Him. The next day He came around in a bus-driver's uniform. That was no good either. The next day it was a telegraph messenger boy, and the day after that in a garbage collector's uniform, all white and new. "You'd better marry me today," He warned Her, "because they've run out of uni-

forms at the masquerade store, and tomorrow I'm coming around in a nudist uniform."

269. He was rather older than She was, but He proposed one night, telling Her that He wanted to marry Her because He knew She was just like Her young widowed mother, whom He thought of as the finest type of woman, lovely, refined, noble. . . . "I think you're in love with mother, not me," She told Him. He looked startled, and then slapped His thigh. "By Jove," He said, "I believe you're right. Do you think she'll have me?"

270. Both He and His brother were in love with Her, but She chose the brother. Then the war came, and the engaged brother was wounded in action, and died in the hospital. He came to see Her to cheer Her up, and found Her reading a letter from his brother; the last letter. She gave it to Him without a word. It read: "Dear Jack: I took something away from you that I want you to have. Please marry Louise, because I know you love her. If you have any kids, name one after me."

271. "How do the people ever stand it, living on farms?" She wanted to know. "Don't they go crazy night after night with no movies or anything to go to?" "Oh, there's usually a movie somewhere around," He assured Her, "but mostly they stay home and love their wives, just the way I would if you'd marry me."

272. They both liked birds and kept pigeons on their roof-

tops, which adjoined. They would exercise their birds with a long pole to direct their flight every evening. He was better at it than She was, and got all Her birds to fly with His and come back to His cotes. Finally She had no birds left at all, and began to shout angrily at Him from across the roofs. "I'll tell you how to get all your birds back, honey," He said. "How?" She wanted to know. "Marry me, and you'll get mine, too."

273.   He didn't wear glasses but She did. One night He told Her He knew all about eyes and could look at Hers and give Her some good advice. He took off Her glasses and made Her look right at Him. "What do you see?" He asked. "A man," She laughed. "See," He told Her, "that's what's the matter with your eyes. You're looking right at your future husband and you don't know it." She was glad She had Her glasses off then, because kissing is nicer without them on.

274.   He was kind of priggish, but then so was She and they made a wonderful pair. They went to see the Angna Enters dance recital, because it as so cultured, but when the dancers began doing a harem squirm, He got very red in the face, put on His hat and took Her by the arm and left. "Why did we leave?" She wanted to know. "I don't think an exhibition like that is any place for my future wife," He announced. She had been picking up valuable hints She thought, but girls seldom argue with a man when He's proposing.

275. He was a very different type, always swearing and curs-ing, and while She was modern and didn't give a damn, She was worried that He would do it in front of Her mother, and cause a fuss. So she decided to wean Him away from the habit by showing Him how it sounded. One night She dropped a dish on purpose and broke it, and then began swearing: "'?!! !)- the **... ...& ...&...'!!) thing! !" She remarked. "Darling," He laughed, "you have the words, but not the tune. Let's get mar-ried, and I'll show you how swearing is really done."

276. She managed His office for Him, and He fell terribly in love with Her. "You're so practical," He told Her one day. "See if you can solve this difficulty for me. I love you so much it hurts, but I can't decide whether to marry you and let my business go to ruin without you, or keep you in my business and ruin my life." "Very simple," She said. "Marry me and give me a share in the business, and then I'll feel it's to my interest to keep it going good when I'm not too busy being your wife."

277. She went away for a long visit, and when She got back everybody she met on the street kept congratulating Her, but She couldn't figure out what for. Then He came over, and cas-ually explained that He had told everybody they were going to be married. "But how do you know I want to get married?" She said. "I don't," He admitted, "that's the whole idea. This way you've got to marry me, because if you don't everybody will think you broke your engagement, and gossip will start."

278.   They were boss and stenographer, and they went to a distant city to a conference. At the hotel desk, He was going to engage two rooms, but the clerk greeted them suavely with: "A double room for you and your wife, Sir? Yes, Sir. We have one very nice one left." They began to laugh, and He said, "Well, why not? Give us the room, and then tell us where the nearest minister is. There's a little detail we ought to attend to first."

279.   They were coming home from college on a train, and they kept passing towns where the houses had "For Rent" signs on them. "I'll bet you could rent a house cheap in some of these towns," She remarked. "I'll bet you could too," He agreed, "but who'd clean it? Do they rent out wives with them?" "No," She said, "you've got to get your own." "Are you going to be busy for the next fifty years?" He asked. "I hope so, darling," She smiled.

280.   He was making a wonderful record in the office because He never made a mistake, but the other employees hated Him for it. One day He made a bad mistake, about which only She knew. "If you don't tell, I can have it fixed by Monday," He told Her. "What difference does it make to me?" She asked. "Oh, nothing," He said; "only seeing that I was going to propose to you as soon as I get that raise they promised me, I should think you wouldn't want me to get fired just yet." "Fresh!" she said; and married him.

281. They were talking about their ambitions in life. "I in-tend to make a little dough," He said, "and buy a chicken farm." "Oh no you're not," She objected quickly; "I hate liv-ing on farms." "Wait a minute," He laughed; "don't I have to propose first, before you get so darned bossy?"

282. "Do you believe in trial-marriage?" He asked Her. "No" She said; "I believe in taking a chance on the real thing. I think a person probably doesn't try as hard to make a go of it if they think they can get out of it any time at all." "You've got the right idea," He admitted. "Will you take the chance with me?"

283. They were sitting in a porch swing, and He looked thoughtful. She said: "What are you sitting so far away for? Come on over here, and pay some attention to me." He moved over sidewise, and the sudden weight at that end broke the chain and down came the swing with them in a heap. "Well I didn't mean smother me!" She laughed; "let me up." "I'd like to smother you with kisses," He told Her, "and I won't let you up until you promise to let me." "All right," She said. "How long will it take?" "The rest of your life, at least," He as-sured her.

284. They attended a bridal shower for a girl friend of Her's who was to be married in two months. "I wonder what it's like," She mused on the way home. "What?" He asked, "being married?" "No, knowing you're going to be married in two

months." "It's easy to find out," He told Her. "Just say the word.
Only make it sooner than two months."

285.   They were eating sliced apples dipped in honey, giving
the sweet slices to each other with their mouths when Her
mother walked in. "What's going on?" She laughed. "We're
pretending we're Eskimos with our hands frozen, and feeding
each other this way," He explained readily. "I only hope Papa
Eskimo doesn't come home and find you playing like this," Her
mother warned. "Oh, it's all right," He said; "we're getting
married." Her mother looked surprised, "When was that decided on?" She wanted to know. "Right now," He admitted.
"I found out she tastes sweeter than the honey does, so I think
I'll keep her for myself." "Don't I have anything to say about
this?" She began objecting. "Sure," He told Her, filling her
mouth with apple; "You get to say 'Yes.'"

286.   Her family was very rich and She was used to wearing
a pair of silk stockings only once and then giving them to the
maid. Then things changed and eventually She was down to
Her last pair of nylons. "Darling," He told Her; "don't let it
worry you. I'd rather look at your legs with nothing on them at
all than at Marlene Dietrich's with diamonds in the dimples of
her knees." "Yes," She sobbed, "but for how long?" "Let's
begin small," He suggested. "Try me for about twenty years,
and then decide."

287. She was trying to grow a tomato plant in Her window box, but between the wind and the sun and the rain and the bugs, it was always on the verge of dying. He knew all about plants and She kept asking His advice. Finally He couldn't help laughing at Her lonely little tomato plant. "I'll tell you what," He said; "if you'll forget about that sad little plant long enough to marry me, I'll paper the house with tomatoes if you like."

288. They worked in a sample testing department, and He began noticing painted letters on the samples She passed to Him which He didn't recognize as testing marks. Finally He realized that they spelled out a message: "I love you, you big dumb-bell." He got hold of some samples and marked them, and passed them back to Her, saying on them, letter by letter: "I love you twice as much; let's get married and spell it out in kisses."

289. He had a bad reputation as a wolf, and She was rather nervous on their dates. Still, He never got rough, and She kept going out. One night, in the car, He said: "Listen I want to ask you something, but I don't know how you'll take it?" "What is it?" She asked. "I don't want you to think I ask every girl a thing like this," He went on, "I've really got to like a girl a lot first." She began to get scared. "What do you want to ask me, Jerry?" She said. "What I mean is, I like you and you like me, so why don't we—aw, you know what I mean." "I think I do," She said angrily, "and you can let me right out of this car." He

looked amazed. "Gee," He said, "I've heard of girls turning down proposals, but I never heard of them getting mad." "Proposal," She said, "I thought it was a proposition!"

290. She decided She was getting plump and went on a diet. She had enough strength of character to exercise and diet rigorously, and began losing weight fast. Finally He began to object. "But I liked you the way you were. You're more fun to hug when you're a little plump." But She insisted She was going to continue for two more weeks. "Hey," He said, alarmed; "I think I'd better marry you before you dwindle to nothing and disappear."

291. They stopped in front of the hall mirror on their way to a show. "We make a nice combination, don't we," She said. "Yep," He agreed, "too nice to break up. Let's get married and preserve it."

292. She was wearing a hat with a long veil. The wind blew it and tangled it in the buttons of his coat. "I know I'm attached to you," He said; "but I couldn't be sure till now that you were attached to me too. I wish it could last forever." "Is that a proposal," She asked? "If it isn't it's a good imitation, isn't it?" said He.

293. He was in the insurance business, and one night He brought around a policy for Her to see. It was made out on

Her heart, and guaranteed Her heart against any pain, inse-
curity, or unhappiness as long as it was left in the keeping of
the "party of the second part." "Who is this 'party of the
second part'?" She wanted to know. "That's me, darling," He
said; "and that policy is good for a lifetime."

294. She liked pets, and maintained a small menagerie in her
home. She had a parrot, a canary, a pair of lovebirds, a glass
tank of fishes, a cat, and a dog. He had been wanting to pop
the question for a long time but knew he'd have to take her
with her pets. One day he arrived with three new cages, a metal
stand for a fish tank, a cushion and a dog bed. He said, "I
thought the pets would like new things, too, like a bride does."

295. He was from another town and had just met Her a few
weeks before. "You know," He said, "I have to go back pretty
soon, and the fellows will ask me whether the girls were nice
in this town. How about coming back with me and showing
them in person." "I'd like to," She said, "but my family might
object." "Family nothing," He said, "from now on I want to
be your whole family."

296. Her mother was describing her wedding to Him. She
sat there starry eyed thinking about how beautiful it had been.
Finally She turned to Him and said, "And when do you expect
to get married?" "On your daughter's wedding day, I hope,"
He answered, squeezing Her hand covertly.

297.   Three of her girl friends had gotten married within a year. "Strange," He said, "that the whole quartet should fall for Dan Cupid's line of blarney in so short a time." "Quartet? You mean trio," She corrected. "No, I mean quartet," He insisted. "You're getting married next, in case you don't know it; and to me."

298.   They were both in engineering school, and the students were all very serious. She loved Him dearly, but He was so serious all the time, She didn't know how to show it without annoying Him. Just when She was about ready to give up, He turned up one evening at her room with an engineer's transit— that thing that looks like a telescope on a tripod—and began sighting in all directions in her little room. "What on earth are you doing?" She wanted to know. "Orders, lady," He said, imitating a busy engineer; "we're laying the foundations for your married life, and I'm here to put in the groundwork."

299.   Her boy-friend was the captain of a boat on the Great Lakes. "Don't you get lonesome out there when the rain and snow come down?" She asked. "I sure do," He said, "and I'd marry you and take you along if it weren't such an awful life for a woman." "Well, I could have a little house by the lake edge and wait for you there," She suggested, "that is, if you really want me." "Want you?" He shouted, "my tongue is hanging out a yard I want you so!"

300. The radiator wouldn't bring up any heat while he was visiting, and she banged on it with a book-end, but nothing happened. "The janitor must be out," She apologized. "It's all right," He said. "Come on over here and I'll hug you till you're good and warm." "Uh uh," She objected. "I might get to like it, and then what would I do when you went away." "Why should I go away?" He said. "If you like the sample, you can marry me, and we'll live without a furnace."

301. She wanted to buy a picture for her place, and He was an artist with an exhibition on a street corner in the Bohemian part of town. "What kind of a picture did you want?" He asked when She had looked over all His without finding any She liked. "Oh, I don't know," She admitted cutely, "But I'll know it when I see it." "That's the way I've always felt about a wife," He agreed; "that I'll know her when I see her; and you're the one. How about seeing me every day for two weeks and then deciding whether you could stand me for the rest of your life?"

302. She was a hostess on an air-liner, and He was going to Washington on a hurried trip for the firm He worked for. It was His first ride in a plane, and He got terribly sick. She was very solicitous, with a little paper container for Him to be sick into, and He was so grateful that He made a point of getting on the plane with Her coming back. This time He wasn't sick, and He made a date. After seeing her steady for

a few months, He said one day: "Meeting you up in the sky that day when I needed help so much made me think of you as an angel. Will you come and live in my house forever angel?"

303.   "Have you told your mother yet that we have to get married?" He asked Her. "No!" She cried, shocked and frightened; *"Do* we have to?" "Positively," He assured Her. "Otherwise I'll go crazy."

304.   He had known Her for several months, but had not had many dates with Her. One night He decided She was meant for Him, and went over to tell Her. She wasn't home, so He sat down on the steps to wait. After about three hours She came home—with another man escorting Her. Then, to Her escort's surprise, and Her's, He blurted out: "We're getting married. I'm not going to sit around on your doorstep till all hours of the night waiting to propose, only to have you come home with another man!"

305.   He got a post-card from a friend in South America, asking how He was, and whether He had any new "heart-throbs." He showed it to Her, and She smiled. "Well, do you have any new ones?" She asked. "No," He admitted, "same old heart-throb I've always had. You. When are you going to marry me, and let my heart get back to normal?"

306.   He was going away for a while and at the station where She was seeing Him off He asked Her to promise to wait for Him.   When She promised, He took out a diamond ring and slipped it on the third finger of Her right hand.   "My right hand?" She asked.   "That's for friendship."   "Friendship nothing!" He told Her;   "right hand, left hand, or big toe, that ring is for marriage!"

307.   They were sitting on the porch when the baby next door began to howl like mad.   "Do you like children?" She asked hopefully.   "Nope, I hate 'em," He admitted.   "You get to like them, though," She ventured.   "If they were yours and mine maybe I would," He said.   "But what if you wouldn't?" She insisted.   "Then we'd sell them to the gypsies and get a divorce " He laughed.

308.   He knew her very well and used to drop over often without any warning.   One day She wasn't there and He felt such a let-down when He missed Her greeting and Her smile and kiss that He couldn't wait for Her to get back.   When She did He took Her in his arms and said: "Darling, the thrill of having you home ready to greet me is the biggest thing in my life.   Will you let me make it permanent?"

309.   She was an old-fashioned girl, and was up on the language of postage-stamps and flowers and things like that.   "Would you understand any kind of message hidden in the

way the postage-stamps are put on an envelope?" He asked. "Certainly," She said. And the next day She got an enormous envelope in the mail, with stamps of all colors spelling out in big letters: I LOVE YOU—MARRY ME?

310.   "If I had to go away for ten years, would you still love me when I got back?" She asked Him. "Sure I would," He told Her. "Are you going away?" "No, it was just a hypo-thetical question," She admitted. "Now it's my turn," He said. "If I asked you to marry me, would you?" "Sure I would," She said, "but I suppose now you're going to tell me it's just another hypothetical question." "The heck it is!" He said. "I never meant anything so much in my life!"

311.   He always wore a ring on His baby finger, and She used to kid him about it. Finally one day He said, "That ring isn't being worn for an ornament; it was my mother's ring and she told me to give it to the girl I thought could take her place in my heart." "Have you met a girl like that?" She asked, suddenly serious. "No," He confessed, "but you could go right alongside of her if you want to. You'd make a swell mother for somebody's kids, and I'd like them to be mine."

312.   The men in His family all went bald early, and He was twenty-eight. "Darling," He told Her one day; "if you want a husband who still has some hair, we'd better get mar-ried pretty soon." "I'm not marrying you for your hair," She said, "but I'm glad you're worrying about what I like."

313.   He was a spendthrift, and She decided to show Him how
silly it was by an object lesson.   One night she decided was
Leap Year night, and She was going to take Him out and pay
for everything.   She took cabs all over the place, tipped in
quarters and half-dollars for every little thing, ordered a big
expensive dinner, and then danced with Him while it got cold,
bought Him an enormous boutonniere from the giggling
flower-girl, and then insisted on getting him a beautiful and
useless key-chain.   Finally he began to object.   "Well that's
the way you spend your money," She said.   "What you need
is a keeper!"   "You're doing a pretty good job," He said.   "How
about a life-time contract?   Just let me keep about two bucks
out of my pay each week to waste, so I'll feel like a man."

314.   He showed Her a gold coin that His grandfather had
shot a hole through neatly years before, in the bad old days of
the West.   "Why don't you have a ring made out of it," She
said; "but no, I suppose not.   Gold rings aren't very fashion-
able."   "They are as wedding rings," he told her, slipping the
pierced coin over her finger as far as it would go.

315.   They had a three-day marriage law in the state, and when
a friend asked Him to take his girl and him to the next state in
His car to get married, He was glad to do so, and took along His
girl to help out as a witness.   After the ceremony, He looked
at Her, and She looked at Him, and the same thought sprang

in both their minds. "What do you say we get married and save gasoline and tires instead of coming down here later when we get up the courage." "I've got the courage now," She said.

316.   They met at a roller skating rink. One day after going with each other for only a short while, She got a package in the mail, containing a pair of skates, and a note saying: "Cinderella dropped a slipper, and these are skates I know. But if they fit you, you're the wife for me." Roller Skates, as every-one knows, can be adjusted to fit every foot, as She told Him next time She saw him. "Sure," He said, "but it isn't your foot I love; it's you, and it's you I want to marry."

317.   They were listening to a lecture on truth, and when they left He said to Her, "Now tell the truth, what are you waiting for to marry me?" "The truth?" She asked. "The truth," He insisted. "Well," She said with a sigh, "I was only waiting for you to ask me."

318.   Both He and Her brother were ardent short-wave radio operators, and they used their sets as a sort of telephone between their houses. One day Her brother got Her into a discussion of marriage in his "ham-shack" where his set was, and asked Her if She'd marry Her boy-friend if He asked. "Would I?" She said. "I'd marry him so fast it would singe His eyelashes." Her brother snapped a switch and She suddenly heard Her boy-friend's voice saying: "That's all I want to know. I'll take my chances on the eyelashes."

319. He was famous for the Texas tall-tales He could tell, and not a week went by without a new whopper about Paul Bunyan's blue ox, or Snake-Tooth Sam and his trained rattler. One day at a party, He was called on to tell the biggest lie He could think of. "Well," He said, "I could tell about the Oregon rainstorm where the rain fell in the spigot of my old man's barrel faster than He could pour it out both ends, or I could tell about the blizzard up in Michigan that caught me shingling the roof, and I shingled three feet out onto the frozen air and then back onto the roof again without knowing it; but the really biggest lie I know would be to say that I don't love Mary-Jane Allison, and I don't want to marry her."

320. There was a big iron fence between their houses, put up by the last owner, and He used to vault over it to visit with Her. One day He miscalculated, and ripped His pants right down the seam, going over the iron pickets. "What's the matter," She said when She got Her laughter under control; "are you losing your grip?" "No," He said, "it's just that I love you so much I can't eat my vitamins. How about marrying me and feeding me spinach till I get my strength back."

321. Rationing was beginning to bother both of them. He had stood in line for hours to get a ration book, and then stood in line hours more to get the things He needed. When finished He was good and angry, and He strode over to Her house and began kissing Her over and over. "What's got into you, Art?"

She said. "Are you afraid I won't be here to kiss tomorrow."
"I'm afraid they'll be rationing kisses by then," He said, "And
I'm stocking up. Maybe I even ought to marry you and be sure
of a supply for the next bunch of years." "Maybe," She said.
"Got your mind made up yet?" "I'll say!" He said.

322.   The girls were having fun on Hallowe'en looking into a
mirror in a dark room with one candle to see the face of the man
they would marry. When it came Her turn, and She went into
the dark room, to Her surprise there really *was* a face in the
mirror, and not only that but two arms went around Her, and
She found herself being thoroughly kissed by the man She was
in love with. "How did you get in here?" She demanded.
"It's magic," He said. "I'm the man you're going to marry.
The mirror says so. Are you going to ask questions, or are you
going to name the day, and kiss me again?"

323.   She had taken up archery at a summer camp, but He
laughed it off as simple. "I'll bet you could never even hit
the target," She insisted angrily. "Will you pay a forfeit if I
do?" He asked. She agreed, and He went out to the range with
Her, and to her amazement put three arrows into the gold center
one after the other. "You win," She admitted; "but tell me two
things: A—was that an accident? B—what's the forfeit?"
"A—," He said, "I used to be champ at archery in the boy-
scouts. B—you've got to marry me." She picked up the bow
and kissed it. "This must be Dan Cupid's own," She said.

324. He was very thin. "Why you're so thin," She said, "when you stand sideways I can't see you." "That's all right," He said. "When we're married it'll make it just so much easier for me to sneak out to play cards." "You won't have to sneak out," She said; "I can play cards too—pinochle or poker, which do you prefer?" "I really prefer to play for money," He said; "but I guess playing for kisses would be fun too."

325. Her shoelace came untied while they were out walking, and He kneeled on one knee in front of Her to fix it. But He didn't get up then. "While I'm here," He said, "I may as well take the opportunity of proposing to you in the good old-fashioned style." "And I may as well accept in the same old-fashioned style," She said, lifting him up by the chin to kiss him.

326. She had been going with Him a long time, and He had never popped the question. Thinking to give Him a subtle hint, She sent Him a humorous valentine on Valentine's Day, with a poem on it about a man who takes up all of the girl's time without ever proposing. But the same day She mailed it off, what was Her embarrassment to get a gorgeous lace and satin valentine in the following mail, addressed "To My Darling Little Wife," to which He added in ink the words: "—To Be."

327. He was a bill collector and had to collect a bill from Her that a younger brother of Hers had incurred. He called every week for three months before it was finally paid off. "Young

lady," He told Her, "I admire the honesty with which you've paid off a debt that wasn't even your own. But I'm surprised that you're not making any effort to satisfy the other honest debt that's been your sole responsibility." "Why, what debt do you mean," She asked? "I mean you stole my heart," He said; "And I think it would be only right for you to give me yours in return—for keeps."

328.   She had a beautiful Maltese cat with rich beautiful fur. Like all cats it was very cold in its affections, but it went crazy over Her boy-friend and would rub against Him and roll over for Him every time He came. "How do you do it," She finally asked. "It's easy," He admitted. "I put cat-nip in my pants cuffs. I've been hoping you'd decide that if even a creature with a nasty disposition like that cat could love me, a lovely creature like you could love me too. I know it's silly and dishonest, but I'd do even worse things to get you for my wife."

329.   She was very petite, and very cute, and He adored Her, being a big hulking brute of a man. Finally He got around to asking Her to marry Him. "Oh, I don't know," She said petulantly. "I wouldn't want a husband that I can order around the way I do with you." "So that's how it is," He mused, "you like cave-man stuff. And here I've been treating you so gentle because I thought a puff of air would break you in half. Well then . . . " And He slapped Her rudely just below the small of Her back so hard that it nearly threw Her across the room.

Then He picked Her up by the waist, and pulled Her hair, and tucked Her under His arm, and started off with Her. "Listen here, you peanut-sized tomato," He told Her, "we're going to a preacher and get married right now; and one word out of you and I'll bat your ears into the middle of next week." "I didn't say a word," She said meekly.

330.   Her father came into the parlor in his night-shirt, carrying a clock and a scythe one night very late while He and She were holding hands in the dim light of one lamp. "Why father," She exclaimed, "what on earth are you dressed up for?" "I'm supposed to be Old Man Time," said Her father. "I can't get no sleep with you two makin' all them kissin' noises in the parlor. Why don't you get married and spoon around in your own house." They burst out laughing and agreed to do so immediately.

331.   He had been a bachelor for a long time, and cooked extremely well. One day He served Her a wonderful supper, from soup to nuts, and featuring a splendid steak rubbed with garlic and a dab of mustard. "You're a wonderful cook," She told Him. "If you could only sew and clean I'd marry you." "Well who do you suppose does my sewing and cleaning if not me?" He asked. "Marry me, and I'll teach you how it's done." Clever bachelor!

332.   Her mother was always complaining about Her getting

home late, and used to lock Her out if She came in after midnight. He resented that very much. "If you were going to do anything bad, you could do it just as well at 8:30," He insisted. One night when He brought Her home only to have Her find She was locked out, He got very angry. "Let's teach them a lesson," He said. "Instead of you begging to be let in, the way they want, let's you and me drive out on the highway over the state line and wake up one of those marrying preachers and get married. Then you can come home any time you damn well please."

333.   It was a windy, rainy day and She ran into Him and tore His umbrella with Hers. "I suppose I ought to get sore," He said, "but what can you expect from a woman?" That made her angry. "All you can expect from a woman is to have a son like you," She snapped. Months later, when their acquaintance had been going on for some time after that bad beginning, He reminded Her of it. "And can I expect a woman to want a husband like me too," He asked. "Not if you go around speaking to strange women in the street," She laughed.

334.   He was shy to the point of being tongue-tied, and one night He began stammering and stuttering pathetically. "What are you trying to say darling," She asked "That you love me?" "Uh-huh!" He agreed, and began to stutter some more. "And that you want to marry me," She went on. He could only nod in assent. "All right, I'll marry you," She said. His face lighted

up happily. "Whew," He said. "I never thought I'd get that off my chest, but I did, didn't I?"

335.   They were crossing traffic when a cop began to bawl them out for crossing against the lights. He took the bawling out meekly, and later She berated Him for that. "Why didn't you talk back to him?" She asked. "I've never had any practice at being called down," He said, "and I didn't know how to act. Maybe I'd better marry you and get to know all the answers."

336.   She was a lifeguard at a beach and He found that very funny, being twice as big as She was. "Could you save me if I were drowning?" He asked Her, after having spent practically every day with Her all summer. "I sure could," She maintained. "Well, start now," He said, plunging into the water "I'm going to drown myself if you don't promise to marry me." "All right," She shouted after Him and He paddled away powerfully, "I'll marry you; but only because I don't want to get my bathing suit wet this close to quitting time."

337.   She was enthusing about the handsome actors in the movies, especially about their old-world charm, so one night He showed up in an Inverness cape, wearing a black Homburg hat, and a monocle, and carrying a cane. "I say there, my deah young woman," He said to Her, in the phoniest British accent possible; "do you suppose you could take off an hour and marry me? In my bored aristocratic way I'm teddibly in love with you,

you know." "Take off that crazy outfit, you loon," She laughed, "Or I'll never marry you."

338.   They were pickling cucumbers and She was taking great care with it. "You have to do it just right," She explained to Him, "or they won't come out properly at all." "I have the same darn trouble," He said, seeing his chance. "I want to propose to you, but I'm sure it has to be done just right, or it won't come out properly at all." "Just any old way will do, darling," She told Him; "proposing and pickles are two different things."

339.   He was visiting Her and She was still dressing when He arrived, so He started to play with Her little niece, ending by riding around on her kiddy-car, with His knees sticking out ridiculously. Suddenly He was aware that She had come down and was watching Him. "Darling," He said, turning to Her; "this is the Magic Horse whereof the Arabian Nights speak. Mount and ride with me into the heaven of matrimony. How about it, toots." She pushed Him over with Her foot, and He caught Her ankle and brought Her down on top of Him. "Any day," She said, "but not on Dotty's kiddy-car."

340.   The tailor had forgotten to make cuffs on His new pants, and She offered to. She gave Him her dressing gown to wear while She fixed the pants, but She cut off the first one too short, and then cut off the other leg even shorter trying to make it

match. Before she was finished they were knee length. She was almost in tears. "And I so wanted to make a good impression," She cried, "and show you what a good wife I'd make." "It's all right," He soothed Her, "sew buttons on them and we'll use them for knee-britches for our first baby if it's a boy."

341.   They were at the zoo and She kept Him watching the monkeys with Her for half an hour. "Let's go, darling, I can't stand the smell," He said. "You could if you loved me," She said. "If I could stand that kind of a smell," He countered, "I'd love a monkey. This way I'm only going to marry one." "You are not!" She snapped. "So you admit you're a monkey!" He laughed. They're still squabbling.

342.   They went into a jewelry store to have a date engraved in a class ring, but the jeweler thought they were shopping for an engagement ring and kept pulling out trays of them. "I see this is a frame-up," He said at last. "How much are you paying this jeweler to keep hinting that I ought to propose? Lord knows I want to marry you, but I can't afford a ring." "We can arrange easy terms, Sir," said the jeweler, helpfully. "I give up," He said. "Ring out, wild bells!"

343.   The tile roof of Her house leaked, and She used to call Him over each time to fix it, as His apartment was just next door. One day She felt the water dripping onto Her nose, but looking outside She saw the sunshine. She went up on the roof

and found Him there pouring water into Her apartment. "I
can't help it," He admitted, "I love you so much I keep wanting
to find excuses to come over to your apartment. Let's get
married." "I suppose it's the best thing to do," She agreed,
"or I'll wake up some night afloat."

344.   She was having Her fortunte told, and the fortune-teller
described as the man She was going to marry a man completely
opposite in size, color of hair, age, and everything to Her current
boy-friend. She told Him about it with a laugh. "That proves
you can't trust fortune-tellers, doesn't it?" She said. "I don't
know," He said; "and I'm not going to take any chances.
I'm going to marry you myself before the guy she described
comes along."

345.   They were having dinner in a fine restaurant at his
insistence; complete with champagne. He tried to take the cork
out of the bottle himself, and the champagne spilled all over
him and messed his clothes. "Don't cry," She said, seeing how
unhappy He looked. "I'm sure dry-cleaning will fix your suit."
"It isn't my suit I'm worried about," He said. "It's that I brought
you here to propose to you and now I look like a bum I'm sure
you'll say no." "Try me, and see," She suggested softly.

346.   When Christmas came, She waited too long and couldn't
get a tree in the end. And then He showed up bearing an
enormous fir tree. "What on earth will I do with it," She wailed

when He brought it in, for it took up the whole apartment.
"Well, with this—" and He tore off a branch, "we'll make a
Christmas tree," He said, and He threw the rest out the back
window. "And with the rest I'm going to build you a house
when spring comes and marry you."

347.   "Do you know what makes some girls into old maids,"
He asked. "No," She said. "That's correct," He said; "So see to
it that you say yes. Will you marry me?"

348.   She could never pronounce "handkerchief," and always
used to say "hanchekief." "The next time you say 'hanchekief'
instead of handkerchief," He told Her; "you're going to have to
marry me." "Well if that's how it is," She said, "I don't care if
I never say hanchekief—I mean handkerchief—again." But he
was there kissing He before She even finished.

349.   "Have you got an hour to spare," He asked Her over
the phone. "Yes, sure," She said. "Well then put on a cute
dress and some make up and hurry over to this address," He
went on, giving Her an address, "I want you to vamp a guy
for me; it'll save me some money." Rather puzzled she went to
the address, only to find it was a church. "Where's the man?"
She asked. "He's inside," He whispered in a very conspiratorial
way. "It's the minister. He wants to charge five bucks to marry
us, but if you give him a nice smile I think he might come down
to three bucks." "Is that cash?" She asked, "or will cigar coupons

do?" "Not if we want a real marriage," He said; "and I for one, do."

350.   She was always saying She wouldn't marry Him if He were the last man in the world. Finally one day He said: "If I were the last man in the world you wouldn't have a chance. There'd be a line of women three hundred miles long waiting to marry me, and the way I calculate it, if the line was alphabetical, you'd be three miles past Cleveland. Meanwhile, if you want to marry me now, you're the only one in line at the present time."

351.   He sent Her a letter saying: "I can't figure it out: G.K.F. or G.M.F." "What was your letter about?" She asked when She saw Him next. "Who are G.K.F. and G.M.F.?" "Oh that's just something that's troubling me," He said. "It means Get Kissed First? or Get Married First?" "Take your time and have both," She laughed.

352.   She had a habit of saying: "Are you kidding?" One night He said to Her, "You know, Daisy, I'm thinking of getting married." "Are you kidding?" She said. "No, I'm serious. I'm thinking of getting married to you, as a matter of fact." "Are you kidding?" She said. "Well, figure it out for yourself," He went on, pulling out a ring and a blank license. "All you have to do is put this on and help me fill this in." "Are you kidding?" She said, a little weakly. "Not a bit," He said. "But there's one thing: when the minister says: 'Do you promise to

love, honor, and oh-baby?' or whatever He says; if you open your mouth and say 'Are you kidding', so help me I'll murder you." "Are you kidding?" She said.

353.   He brought Her roses, and began pulling out the petals one by one and strewing the floor with them. "Oh, don't do that," She said, "why spoil them; they're so pretty." "I'm not spoiling them," He said angrily; "I'm trying to find one that comes out right. She will—she won't—she will—she won't—" "Who are you talking about," She asked. "You," He said. "And what won't I do?" "Won't nothing! You will! You'll marry me if I have to carpet the room with rose-petals proving it."

354.   She was afflicted with hay-fever, and the second year He knew Her when She began sneezing, He began sneezing too. "Oh my," She said, "have you got it too?" "Yes," He said, "I went out and had myself innoculated with it to keep you company." "Oh, you didn't," She said, "It isn't possible." "No," He admitted, "it isn't. But I wanted to. I'm practising for that 'in sickness and in health' stuff in the marriage cere-mony." "Why," She asked coyly, "are you getting married?" "If it's easier to catch you than it's been to catch hay-fever I'm getting married," He said.

355.   They were in the library, talking in whispers. They were arguing about love, and they raised their voices several times

and were hushed by the librarian. Finally He shouted in a loud voice that every one could hear, "All right then, if you won't marry me I'll tear up all the books and kill myself." The librarian pattered over. "Please don't tear up our books," she said; "they're very expensive. And there's a rule against killing yourself in here. Perhaps," and she peered over her glasses, "perhaps if you took the lady to somewhat more romantic surroundings she would be easier to persuade."

356. He was kissing Her one night, which was not unusual for them, but He had his hands tightly around Her neck. "What's that for," She wanted to know; "the new movie technique?" "No," He said. "I want you to marry me, and I'm hoping this way to be able to squeeze out a Yes or choke down a No, as the case may be."

357. She was a very earnest student, but one day crossing the campus He bumped into Her and Her notebooks and papers went flying in all directions. He helped Her pick them up and that was the beginning of their friendship. One day on the way home from classes He took Her books out of Her hands and threw them up in the air in all directions. "Are you crazy?" She said; "you've ruined my assignment for tomorrow." "Oh no I haven't," He said. "Your assignment for tomorrow is to marry me. We're quitting school and going on a one year's honeymoon. My father sent me four thousand dollars, and is going to set us up in a home when we come back."

358.   They were out on a double date in his car, and the couple in the rumble seat had necked for hours without saying a word. Finally He turned around and poked the other man on the shoulder. "Hey, come up for air," He said. The other man looked up and gave Him a sour look. "What's the matter, doesn't your girl neck?" the other man asked. "Sure, but she can talk too," He said. "Well then marry her," said the other man, going back to his girl, "this babe can only kiss." "Next time I'll mind my own business," He said. "Why," asked She, "is his suggestion so bad?" "No, it's wonderful," said He, "but now when I ask you you'll think it wasn't my own idea."

359.   She was looking out the window when He proposed. "Darling," He said, "do you see that street down there?" "Yes," She said. "Well every second man on that street is probably a better catch than me, so it's hard for me to get up the nerve to ask you to marry me." "Do you see that street down there?" She countered. "Yes," He said. "Well, every girl down there is there after those men you mentioned; but I'm up here with you. Does that solve your problem for you?"

360.   The pencil sharpener in the office was broken, and he had a very sharp knife. After watching Her haggle her broken-pointed pencil with her teeth and one edge of a scissors for a while, He came over and said: "Honeybunch, I hope you know more about cooking than you do about sharpening pencils, because I'm going to marry you as soon as I finish doing it

for you." So saying He pulled out his knife and created a long artistic point on the offending pencil. "What do you say?" He asked. "I say if cooking could be done with a knife my half of this marriage would be as easy as yours," She smiled. "But even as it is I'm willing."

361. They were eating watermelon in a cafeteria, and He refused to eat with a knife and fork, but picked up a whole slab of it and began digging into it with His front teeth. "You put that down, or I'll leave," She said. "I never saw such table manners in my life." "Well," He said, wiping His mouth on His sleeve; "either get used to them or change them because you're going to be seeing them over the breakfast table for the rest of your life."

362. Her mother gave Her a piece of ivory-colored veiling, and She was wondering what to do with it. "I could make the most attractive little hat-veil out of it," She told him; "or it would make a fascinator and that's very stylish." "Listen," He said, "I don't want you to go around fascinating people or being attractive to anybody else but me. Maybe you'd better make a wedding veil out of that yellow mosquito-netting, and you can fascinate me for years and years."

363. He called Her up in the middle of the night on the telephone. "Do you love me, darling?" He asked. "You know I do," She said, "And I think it's sweet calling me up to tell

me so no matter what time it is." But she didn't think it was so sweet when He kept it up for hours, and didn't let Her get a wink of sleep. Finally, when He realized that next time She would just leave the receiver off the hook, He said: "I'm only trying to show you how convenient it would be for you to marry me. If we were married I wouldn't have to telephone you to tell you how I love you. I could just nudge you."

364.   "Sweetheart," He said. "I know I'm crazy to want to get married. You'll probably nag every hair off my head, and give me twenty cents of my own wages for my weekly allowance, and get me down to a diet of one kiss every two weeks, but I love you so much I can't sleep or eat. Will you marry me?" "I'll marry you," She said, "but why do you make it sound so hopeless?" "Well," He said, "I figure that if I expect the worst, and that's what happens—why, I expected it. And if it turns out good—then I'll be on velvet."

365.   It was a rainy night, one of those days that only a duck could love. John and I were walking home from the movies, huddled close under a makeshift piece of paper. "Baby face," He said, "let's go and do it." "Do what?" I exclaimed in astonishment and surprise. "Let's get married, so we won't have to go out every time we want to hold hands."

Lightning Source UK Ltd.
Milton Keynes UK
UKOW02f2254141116
287663UK00002B/327/P

9 781614 272618